Jim Mellon is an investor and entrepreneur with a flair for establishing successful companies around the globe. His businesses include a listed fund management company, an Asian mining group and an Isle of Man based bank. Burnbrae, his private company, is a substantial landlord in Germany and in the Isle of Man, and also owns Sleepwell Hotels.

Al Chalabi is a business consultant and entrepreneur who has been based in Asia for the past 13 years. He has extensive experience in establishing and growing businesses in developing economies. Currently based in Hong Kong, Al has lived, studied and worked in the UK, Canada, France and the United States.

Top Ten Investments to Beat the Crunch!

Invest Your Way to Success in a Downturn

Jim Mellon and Al Chalabi

CAPSTONE

First published in 2009 by Capstone Publishing Ltd (a Wiley Company)
The Atrium, Southern Gate, Chichester, PO19 8SQ, UK.
www.wileyeurope.com
Email (for orders and customer service enquires): cs-books@wiley.co.uk

Other Wiley Editorial Offices

John Wiley & Sons Inc., 111 River Street, Hoboken, NJ 07030, USA
Jossey-Bass, 989 Market Street, San Francisco, CA 94103-1741, USA
Wiley-VCH Verlag GmbH, Boschstr. 12, D-69469 Weinheim, Germany
John Wiley & Sons Australia Ltd, 42 McDougall Street, Milton, Queensland 4064, Australia
John Wiley & Sons (Asia) Pte Ltd, 2 Clementi Loop #02-01, Jin Xing Distripark, Singapore 129809
John Wiley & Sons Canada Ltd, 22 Worcester Road, Etobicoke, Ontario, Canada M9W 1L1

Wiley also publishes its books in a variety of electronic formats. Some content that appears in print may not be available in electronic books.

Library of Congress Cataloging-in-Publication Data
Mellon, Jim.
  Top ten investments to beat the crunch! : invest your way to success in a downturn / by Jim Mellon and Al Chalabi.
    p. cm.
  Rev. ed. of: The top 10 investments for the next 10 years / Jim Mellon & Al Chalabi. 2008.
  Includes index.
  ISBN 978-1-906465-40-7 (pbk.)
  1. Investments. 2. Finance, Personal. 3. Speculation. I. Chalabi, Al.
  II. Mellon, Jim. Top 10 investments for the next 10 years. III. Title.
  HG4521.M4354 2009
  332.63--dc22

                                                                                    2009008886

A catalogue record for this book is available from the British Library.

ISBN : 978-1-90646-568-1

Typeset in Adobe Caslon Pro by Sparks, Oxford – www.sparkspublishing.com
Printed and bound in Great Britain by TJ International Ltd, Padstow, Cornwall

Substantial discounts on bulk quantities of Capstone books are available to corporations, professional associations and other organizations. For details telephone John Wiley & Sons on (+44) 1243-770441, fax (+44) 1243 770571 or email corporatedevelopment@wiley.co.uk

Contents

Prologue

When we published our first book towards the end of 2005, entitled *Wake Up! Survive and Prosper in the Coming Economic Turmoil*, we were very excited to finally see our hard work over the previous 18 months in bookshops all over the world. The feedback we received from many friends and readers was generally neutral; on the whole they found it very interesting and informative but thought we were being overly pessimistic in our predictions for the global economy and in particular those of developed nations of the US and UK. Wasn't there a little too much Chicken Little in the text, warning everyone that the sky was falling?

Among other things, we predicted that the US housing market would experience great difficulties by 2007; this, we said, would precipitate an end to the credit binge that had engorged Western asset prices. We also made some strident economic forecasts.

Many friends and other commentators asked how could we be so bold as to make statements such as 'major investment banks will go bust and property prices will tumble'. For the many who were caught up in the heady days of credit-fuelled bull markets, our words of warning seemed rather far-fetched – and we received wry, benevolent smiles from a lot of the people we spoke to.

Of course, the optimists who formed the majority of investors as recently as 2007 have been sadly confounded. It is now generally accepted that the world is experiencing the sharpest, most painful contraction in asset prices since the Second World War and almost every economy on the planet is suffering either a marked slowdown in economic growth or outright recession.

The catchwords today have become deflation and – horror of horrors – a replay of the Great Depression of 1929–1933.

In many ways, the reaction of the bull market brigade to our Cassandra-like warnings was understandable. At the time the global economy appeared vibrant, stock markets were on the up and so were property prices. People felt richer and more confident than ever.

Yet all the while we knew – and it wasn't because of our special insight or some magic crystal ball, but because of basic facts staring us in the face – that the longer the party went on, the bigger the hangover was going to be. It was just a question of when the global economy did finally start to nosedive.

We have since then kept readers up-to-date with our 'Wake Up!' newsletter, which we send out via email to subscribers. This newsletter has tried to provide timely commentary on pertinent events as they unfold. It is still available today free of charge. You are welcome to subscribe to it by visiting www.wakeupnewsletter.com.

As the newsletters went out, the economic outlook became ever gloomier. In fact, the speed of the implosion of banks, insurance companies, and the scale of the destruction of wealth has exceeded even our rather pessimistic forecasts.

The severity of the global economic crisis is undeniable. Forecasts for growth, or rather contraction, of major economies get darker by the day. Banks around the world are having huge amounts of taxpayer capital pumped into them in a variety of ways. Jobs are being lost at an unprecedented rate – one forecast is for a global loss of jobs of 50 million in 2009. Car companies and other industries around the world are running bleating to governments for bail outs. Governments are borrowing vast sums to prop up their ailing economies and central banks almost everywhere are trying to prime economic activity by quantitative easing (which in layman's terms means printing money).

The EU member states that experienced the biggest booms are now going through the most spectacular busts. For example, in Latvia's capital Riga, flat prices have fallen 56 per cent since the middle of 2007, according to Balsts, a Latvian property company. The country's economy has contracted by 18 per cent in the past six months alone.

Ireland expects its economy to contract by 4 per cent in 2009 and its current account deficit is forecast to reach an unsustainable 12 per cent of GDP by 2010. Large multinational corporations who used to benefit from Ireland's cheap labour and real estate are now leaving for more competitive European countries, such as Poland.

Spain lost a million jobs in 2008 and is expecting unemployment to rise to 16 per cent by the end of 2009. Worse still, some economists are forecasting a peak unemployment rate of 25 per cent before the economy starts to improve. Spain became too reliant on property and tourism, both of which have burst. Over the past decade, Spain's wage inflation has resulted in its labour force being uncompetitive relative to other European countries for the equivalent skills. Standard & Poor's, a rating agency, has just stripped Spain of its AAA credit rating to AA+, citing 'structural weaknesses in the Spanish economy'. This will increase the cost of borrowing for Spain. Other countries in the EU will no doubt follow in due course.

Excluding China, All Major Economies are Expected to Contract in 2009

Country	2009 Real GDP Growth Forecast in January 2008	2009 Real GDP Growth Forecast in January 2009
China	9.8%	7.4%
France	1.9%	−1.0%
Japan	2.0%	−1.7%
US	2.7%	−1.8%
Germany	1.9%	−2.0%
UK	2.0%	−2.2%

Source: Consensus Economics and Bloomberg

Furthermore, the first signs of social tensions directly linked to the economic crisis are emerging: Icelandic pensioners pelting their Parliamentarians with eggs; Russians demanding Putin's removal; Greek youth rioting; and protectionist sentiment – the huge spectre of the 1930s re-emerging in many countries.

But to backtrack a bit; by the start of 2007, we were more sure than ever that we were getting very close to the edge of the precipice. So we decided to start writing our second book, the updated version of which you are holding now.

We realized the period of economic turmoil that lay ahead provided unprecedented opportunities for long-term investors. So we set out to identify these opportunities and at the same time explain to readers why saving and investing is so important for their future wellbeing.

As we write this prologue early in 2009, the world looks very different from the one just a year ago. People and governments are in despair. Confidence in the 'system' has been shaken to the core. Without confidence, there can be no growth. Remember our simple equation for growth that we are fond of using to clearly illustrate the requirements for growth:

$$MONEY \times CONFIDENCE = GROWTH$$

To address the 'money' part of the equation, central banks and governments across the world are injecting hundreds of billions of dollars/pounds/euros/yen into their systems. But throwing money at the problem alone does not assure growth if confidence remains at rock bottom levels.

Valuations of major banks have tumbled as they slowly reveal their true exposure to 'toxic' debt, i.e. debt on their balance sheets that has little-to-no chance of being repaid in full, or at the value ascribed to it by the borrower. This is particularly true of the sub-prime and Alt-A borrowers in the US who were, as we described in *Wake Up!*, dicing with death by lending to unqualified borrowers against lousy real estate assets. To compensate for this quantum of loss – unprecedented in human history – banks have been trying to accumulate as much cash as they can get their hands on.

This process is called deleveraging and it is a painful one. Consequently, banks are generally restricting their lending, even to other banks. They are basically operating under the assumption that almost any borrower can default, which intuitively cannot be true.

But it was the bankers who got us into this mess in the first place. The 'light touch' regulatory regimes in the UK and the US, as well as in many other countries, allowed banks to 'leverage up' their balance sheets to ludicrous levels. This process of leverage is what has imperilled the economic structures of many countries, and will lead to long-term painful ruin for some of the smaller players, particularly in the European Union.

Of course, as economies continue to worsen, the chances of more borrowers defaulting increases, which impels banks to hoard more cash. It's a negative spiral that, if left to continue, would lead to the collapse of the entire economy. That is where we are today, approximately.

We are just like everyone else and the temptation to say 'I told you so' is high. So there – we've said it. But we have to admit that although we saw it coming, we didn't see just how bad it would be. We didn't sell our houses, head for the hills or stock up on the baked beans. And while it all looks pretty grim out there as we write this prologue, we are becoming more optimistic.

Yes, optimistic.

We think that a rally in asset prices, fuelled by inflation, is coming and that investors should start preparing themselves for this.

We have been observers of a slowly unfolding train wreck, fuelled by the naked greed of investment bankers and 'normal banks' paying their people according to short-term bonus systems. These bankers, whose activities became far too large relative to their fundamental job of matching borrowers and depositors, were encouraged in their actions by woeful regulatory regimes. Added to this credit-led orgy of excess speculation was the fuel of recycled savings of countries such as China and Japan with large current account surpluses. These savings (known popularly as foreign exchange reserves) went through circuitous but effective means to add to the real estate mania in many Western economies.

China and other countries sold goods to the West, which couldn't be paid for entirely with other goods, so the balance was satisfied by China investing in US government bonds and other Western assets. A neat circularity, but one in which the seeds of destruction were being laid.

This 'surplus' liquidity, supercharged by the 'innovative' techniques of so-called smart bankers, led to the house and other real estate price mania which characterized so much of Western economic growth over the past ten years.

The collapse of this house of cards has landed us in the current mess. Incompetent governments believing that boom and bust cycles had been abolished were complicit also. Men such as Gordon Brown and Alan Greenspan have a lot to answer for in history.

What a catalogue of disasters!

We now observe all the wryly smiling commentators who thought we had it wrong sounding so negative themselves that they must be wearing hair-shirts and crying themselves to sleep. We see newspaper headlines which are so gloomy that alcohol and anti-depressants must surely be the only growth industries.

But we now see something different: silver linings in the black clouds, the blackness of which are more or less dominating just about everyone else's field of vision.

Ladies and gentlemen – we are optimistic for investors and we think that the next two or three years will present exciting opportunities, particularly for those who follow our strategy in *Top Ten Investments* ... This is because:

1 The hard news headlines in major world economies will be awful for all of 2009 and some of 2010.
2 Unemployment will soar, more bankruptcies will happen and for most people in major economies a bleak 18 months awaits.
3 Banks will need more prodding to lend and governments will have to shovel more capital into them.

4 Social unrest will mount in places of high unemployment, particularly in countries with low savings, falling property prices and inflexible monetary policy (e.g. the non-Germanic members of the European Monetary Union). Spain, Portugal, Greece, Ireland, Latvia etc. have a decade of horror ahead of them. Italy and France won't do much better.

5 BUT the sheer scale of government intervention, and exactly the sort of intervention that DIDN'T take place in the 1930s, is going to lead to the opposite of what most people currently think and expect, and that is –

- rising INFLATION in major economies late in 2010;
- rising confidence amongst consumers around the same time;
- a revival in commodity and property prices around the same time; and
- a revival of private equity deals, currently hugely constrained by lack of financing.

This means that for our dear readers, the time to buy will be over the course of 2009 and in early 2010.

The bargains that you will pick up have the capacity to double, treble or even more in a period of rising inflation and massive – and we mean MASSIVE – government subvention. This will be the biggest buying opportunity of our lives.

So from being the guys on the block who were the party poopers a few years ago, we are now taking the opposite view. We think the party will start up again quite soon. It won't last forever, but in a few years a lot of money can be made by the canny and astute.

We are going into a period of inflation, and by 2011 this inflation will be matched by sharply rising global economic growth.

This inflation is necessitated by the desire of major nations to reduce the worth of the debts that they are piling up to rescue their **entire** financial systems. They are going to do this effectively by printing money – they will use debauchery of inflation.

Our investor readers will be well armed. For them, this will be a time of great opportunity. Over the next couple of years they will move from their defensive positions, hidden behind walls of Japanese yen, reduced mortgage balances, etc. to a front foot position in which fortunes can and will be made.

We will be recommending long-term fixed loans against property assets bought in the current distressed times. We will be advocating commodities – nothing too fancy and accessible to all who want to follow us. We will be advocating 'green' investments because that area will be the focus of so much government 'stimulus' investment. And we will be advocating, as always, an **open, flexible approach** and an **open mind** to the subject of investment.

Why we are becoming bullish is because central banks and governments are in such a state of panic. They know that a deflationary spiral of their worst nightmares cannot be allowed to happen and they have been trying all sorts of ways to avert such a catastrophic outcome. But with no money in their own treasuries' coffers, the US and UK governments have to resort to either borrowing money and/or printing it. The amount of money being borrowed is going to lead to some stratospheric fiscal deficits for 2009 and for a good few years after that. The printing of money will of course lead to high (possibly, though unlikely, hyper-inflation), by effectively diluting the purchasing power of money. This is the famous Gresham's Law. Bad money drives out good. Simple but true. Zimbabwe or the Weimar Republic are great examples of that in extremis.

We are by no means implying that Western economies will ever reach Zimbabwean or Weimar Republic levels of inflation, but their example can be used to highlight the impact of inflation on an economy. The US and the UK have decided to effectively print money to get out of the financial gridlock. The theory is that printing cash or fiat money will increase the velocity (flow) of money and encourage banks to lend once more.

Once banks start lending again, the lifeblood of stimulating economic growth (lending) will be restored. But until all banks' balance sheets come clean about how much toxic debt they are exposed to, it is very difficult for governments to determine how much more bail-out money they will have to come up with.

Once money does start to flow again in the economy, there's going to be a lot of it sloshing around chasing the same goods, services and investment opportunities. This is the most delicate point in the recovery, as inflation could start to gather momentum like a loco-motive, forcing central banks to raise interest rates sharply in order to put the brakes on the economy. High interest rates are not good news for those in debt, namely those with mortgages and of course governments themselves, who are lumbering their constituents with unimaginable levels of national debt.

If we look at the US economy's indebtedness, it stands at some $10 trillion. In an era of low interest rates such as now, where the cost of borrowing is, say, 2 per cent, servicing such a debt will cost the US taxpayer around $200 billion every year. Although this is a vast sum of money, it is less than 1.5 per cent of its GDP and doesn't have much of an adverse impact on the overall economy. If inflation rises, then interest rates of course may rise also, and this will increase debt servicing. But here is where the governments of countries such as the UK and the US are tricking the buyers of debt which cur-rently stand at such low levels of interest: they intend – and it's not conspiratorial, just implied – to issue massive amounts of debt (they have to recapitalize their financial systems, bail out the car companies etc.), and to concurrently print money. Overall the inflation-adjusted value of that debt will fall and even if interest rates rise, most of the interest the governments pay will be fixed at low rates for many years to come.

More fool the buyers of US, UK or European debt today. Far from being 'safe havens', these instruments (and they are the biggest finan-cial market in the world – bigger than stocks and shares) are priced to a perfection that doesn't exist. So for our readers we recommend that they get rid of anything other than the shortest duration govern-ment bonds.

Governments are in a high stakes gamble where things are so bad that their primary objectives are to prevent the banking system from total collapse and to get banks to start lending again. What happens after these two objectives are met will depend on how much money the government will have to spend/print and how long this process takes. In any scenario, the prognosis is not looking good for inflation and government debt.

But the situation IS looking pretty good for anyone who can see what the beneficiaries are of the process of debt devaluation and financial recapitalisation: property, commodities and borrowing at fixed rates for long periods of time. Oh, and green investments, as governments everywhere try and 'spend' their way out of recession.

These are exciting and unprecedented times, and certainly the worst economic situation in our lifetimes. We hope that our book serves as a compass to navigate you through these uncharted waters and we hope to see you in calmer seas in a couple of years.

We are optimistic.

Jim Mellon and Al Chalabi
January 2009

Chapter*One*

Why Are We Here?

We have written this book as a pathway and guide to your financial security. Of course, no book on its own can act as the runway lights for such a complex and dynamic topic as an individual's future financial health.

However, we believe that with the ACTIVE PARTICIPATION of our readers, we can get a good way down the road to safely securing the money part of people's lives.

That's a big boast. But it's a boast grounded in a strong belief that **everyone** has it within them to become a successful investor. The trick is to step back from the daily mayhem and noise of stock and bond markets and to THINK about the big picture. And that's what we try to do, and to inspire you to do also, in this book.

To **think**.

To think about where the world is going, where we as individuals are going within it – and to answer a really key question: how on earth am I going to pay for my future once my working years are over?

We as authors speak from personal experiences; we've had plenty of adventures in our investment careers, some good, some bad – and we share the lessons of these with readers. But there's a really important lesson that we try to get across in *Top Ten Investments to Beat the Crunch!*, and that is:

Investment really isn't that difficult.

The layers of complication that appear to make it so are quite often unnecessary. And of course, the recent financial turmoil adds layers of uncertainty to the decision-making process of every investor. But with the correct focus and application, the current volatility in markets could well provide a cheaply-priced springboard to a really great financial future for our readers.

Sometimes, it appears that the professionals who work in the investment business are that bit smarter, more gifted and better positioned to make money than the general public is. Bitter experience for many people shows that this perceived 'superior skill set' is quite often at the expense of their clients. Look at the bozos who have run venerable banks and investment banks into the ground, as an example.

So, our first task in this book is to strip everything back. Peel the onion down to its centre – to the core of the process of investment. This is a key part of our strategy.

In these pages, we aim to demystify the process of investment. We will put down – in plain language – the ways in which we think you can build up a **solid and substantial** nest egg for future years.

We go over the exact ways that part-time investors can go about buying and selling the assets that make up their nest egg.

We have written this book – and have really enjoyed doing so – for people who aren't employed by fund managers or by investment banks or the like. This book is firmly for the oft-ignored 'retail' investor – the individual who wisely wants to invest for the future. It is NOT a book for money folk – quite the opposite.

There is nothing wrong with those financial industry guys, but this book is designed to eat a little bit of their lunch. And most of them have (or rather had) too much food on their plates. To misuse an old saying: it's about time the clients got their own yachts.

Of course, that's a little tongue in cheek. We will try and circumvent the 'professionals' where possible, but sometimes they can serve a very useful and indeed necessary purpose. In this book we will guide you as to when you need to use a broker, a financial advisor or a fund manager, and when you can just do it by yourself – and thereby save money.

The most important thing is the long-term goal: to build up as much money as possible for you over the next ten years and beyond, using careful planning and strategic investment thinking. With this in mind, we take you through a series of chapters about the disciplines of saving, of making a plan, and of thinking clearly about future trends.

We know that for many people investment can appear to be a bit like black magic. We know that the terminology used in the investment world can be complicated; and for this and other reasons people quite often give up on investing on their own. They either end up using savings 'products' that perform poorly or are badly designed for their own specific needs – or worse, they end up doing nothing at all. So, for that reason, we use **plain** language to describe investment essentials. All of us are perfectly capable of creating a portfolio over time that matches our long-term financial needs – partly on our own and partly with the help of professionals.

In this book, which represents the distilled input of 40 cumulative years of investment experience, we aim to give you an 'edge' over the professionals.

We encourage all of you to make your own plans and we try to show you how, with some effort, you can stick to them and get richer than you ever thought possible.

But the word **'effort'** is a key one. Without your active participation, dear reader, this book won't do a lot to help you. Unless you read *Top Ten Investments* and it sparks some new momentum in your own personal financial planning, it will just be a wodge of bound paper on your shelf.

We don't want this book to languish as a 'comfort book', one where people think that somehow, by osmosis or some other, more mystical process, its contents will filter through. They won't.

Although this book is not a 'how to' manual in the sense of a home improvement instruction volume, it does lay out some quite specific steps for you to follow. These include:

1 **Recognition** that time is of the essence if our individual financial futures are to be secured.

2 An **understanding** that frenetic or 'day' trading in markets of whatever type doesn't work – or at least not often.

3 An understanding that carefully thought out and long-range investment strategies **do work**. So it's that long horizon that we should stick to – hence the '10 Years' in our book's title.

4 **Diversification** – a key feature of any successful investment strategy which will be heavily emphasized in subsequent pages.

5 That it is never too late to start – and **today** is as good as any day to kick off your planning. Quite often people put the vital task of financial planning to one side – and the longer they do so the harder it will be to catch up.

Top Ten Investments to Beat the Crunch! has been written to take you through a dynamic process and achieve three main things:

1 *Confront reality* – Are you fully aware of the financial misery that awaits many of us in our future retirements if we don't do some planning and saving NOW? The fact is that many people make false assumptions about who is going to look after them in their old age. Bear in mind, most of us are living longer and will need more care as we get older. We don't mean to scare readers, but putting proverbial heads in the sand won't pay for your retirement years. Nor will, as we detail later, most government or company pension schemes.

2 *Realize action is needed* – You need to do something about it NOW and develop your own investment *BigIdeas*. In our programme, these *BigIdeas* are the cornerstones of successful financial strategies. We need such strategies to counteract the potential financial crises that will confront anyone who doesn't do something about the dangers of insufficient savings – and of over-reliance on government/company pensions.

3 *Plan and implement change* – Set out strategies where you can build your own *MoneyFountains* – and do so in part by using our tailor-made *DiagnosticGrid*. These terms might seem a bit facile

and gimmicky – but the principles behind them are not. We all need to hit the deep seams of treasure in our investment goals – and we won't do so by slavishly following the status quo.

That 'treasure' is our *MoneyFountain* – and the roadmap whereby we deploy our available assets to find the treasure is the *DiagnosticGrid*. These terms will become a lot more meaningful as the book unfolds, we promise you.

In the book we develop the concept of *BigIdeas* as a means of constructing the correct 'portfolio' of investments for your individual needs. We map out, as the title implies, our own ten *BigIdeas* – but we also encourage you to develop your own.

We then describe how *BigIdeas* can be the source of *MoneyFountains* – the investments that run and run – and pump out the long-term profits that will sustain our financial futures.

These *MoneyFountains* are the one or two *BigIdeas* that will be your own 'home runs'. The *MoneyFountains* will differentiate your own portfolios from the also-ran mediocre performance of most 'professionally' run portfolios.

If you can build your very own *MoneyFountain*, then you can wave goodbye to financial worry. That's what this book is designed to help you to do.

Our unique online *DiagnosticGrid* is available to readers to help them construct a mix of investments suited to their own requirements – matching time of life, economic circumstances and dependants.

The combination of *BigIdeas*, *MoneyFountains* and the *DiagnosticGrid* is one that, correctly used and followed, will give you a formidable advantage – the 'edge' over the professionals.

And actually, our programme is quite simple. Read on – and you'll see what we mean. As we said at the outset, ANYONE, given application and discipline, can build a financial future that's worth having.

But first, let us put this book into its context.

Top Ten Investments to Beat the Crunch! is the follow-up to our 2006 book *Wake Up!*[1] in which we outlined some disturbing economic and political factors confronting our world. These factors were ones that we believed would imperil the comfortable post-war prosperity that most of us in the developed world have enjoyed for so long. Sadly, most of our forecasts in that book – a crash in the US and UK housing markets and deteriorating credit conditions, as well as still-mounting tension in the Middle East – have come true. To an even worse extent than we foretold. We are living through the worst global economic crisis since the Second World War and it's tough out there. That having been said, the message of this revised edition of our book is one of guarded optimism. Things are going to get better – and for investors with guts, now is as good a time as we are ever likely to see to begin investing.

Lest anyone think that our world outlook is exclusively gloomy and that we sit permanently swathed in a cloak of despondency, we need to say right at the start that this book is optimistic in tone. Yes, really.

We believe strongly that the following is true:

1 *Anyone* who follows our plan to a reasonable extent will be in a much stronger financial position ten years hence. We haven't written this book to make money, but because we enjoy communicating our thoughts and practical solutions to a wider audience. We really think we can help people with our programme.

2 Notwithstanding the long-term problems facing the world economy, most notably the pension crisis in the developed world, there are considerable grounds for hope. Diligent saving and a bit of application can and will lead to a strong – and long – financial future for those who make the necessary effort.

---

[1] *Wake Up! Survive and Prosper in the Coming Economic Turmoil.* Mellon & Chalabi, Capstone Publishing (A Wiley Company), 2005.

3 *Top Ten Investments to Beat the Crunch!* will act as a useful foundation to savvy financial planning and investment – *BigIdeas* are the bedrock of our thinking in this book. We want our readers to develop their own *BigIdeas* – and we show you how to do so.

4 We are of the firm view that it is never too late to save and never too late to plan. Look especially carefully at the piece on compound interest in this respect.

5 We also KNOW that we live in an era of enormous opportunity – a time of unsurpassed technological development, of widening global trade and development. We occupy this world during a period in which the potential for sustained and profitable development has never been better.

6 We also live in a period of unprecedented challenges; environmental, political and economic. Ironically, it is those very challenges that have provided us with the inspiration for some of our best *BigIdeas*. As just one example, climate change and its abatement offer huge money-making opportunities, which we detail in some depth later on.

Recapping our earlier point that this is the world's golden age of opportunity – albeit a period likely to be interrupted by cyclical downturns – consider this amazing snippet of history:

It is a fact that until 1820 or thereabouts, the world's economy grew at a glacial pace. It has been estimated that during the 800 or so years from 1000 AD to the onset of the Industrial Revolution, the world's overall economic growth averaged about 0.05 per cent per annum, i.e. virtually no growth. Almost all of the world's development beyond a hand-to-mouth rural existence has occurred since 1820.

The commercialization of steam engines, the exploitation of fossil fuels, the improvement in agricultural techniques and the explosion in population growth – all of these have happened in less than 200 years. The world economy is now, excluding the current period of global recession, growing at about **100 times** the rate of its preindustrial period. In other words, the world's economy is growing such that every 15 years or so it is DOUBLING in real terms. That is truly amazing.

We live in the most fortunate – but also, in many ways, the trickiest – of all periods in mankind's history. Don't let yourself be blindsided by current economic woes – they will pass and the world economy will once again grow.

The best is yet to come.

Chapter*Two*

Getting Your House in Order

As we outlined in the introduction, this book is specifically designed to help you understand how you can go about creating a platform from which you can build wealth over the long term. This wealth will allow those who follow our advice to attain financial security, particularly in retirement when our traditional income stream, i.e. our salary, ceases.

Before we delve into the 'how' of building your wealth, it is important to explain the 'why'. We believe the why is compelling and is the primary reason that we decided to write this book (we have assigned a suitably serious title for this next section to explain ...).

Savings Crisis

As some readers might already know, there is a global demographic transformation underway that will have serious consequences to the economies of rich nations in the coming decades. Although we don't plan to go into too much demographic analysis, you need to know that the changes are very real and their economic impact will be felt well within our lifetime. You can read more about the demographic changes in our previous book, entitled *Wake Up!*[1]. These are the key points you need to know:

---

[1] *Wake Up! Survive and Prosper in the Coming Economic Turmoil.* Mellon & Chalabi, Capstone Publishing (A Wiley Company), 2005, pp. 12–18.

- The global population is steadily increasing and is expected to hit the nine billion mark by 2050 (a 50 per cent increase in just 50 years). The irony is that 85 per cent of this growth is from, and will continue to come from, the poor and developing countries. The developed countries are faced with a negligible or, in some cases, negative population growth.
- Modern medicine will continue to allow us to live even longer, so our life expectancy by the time we retire could easily be ten years longer than it is today.
- Improved farming techniques and engineered crops will enable us to feed the growing population, up to a point.
- A large demographic 'bulge', known as baby boomers (those born after World War II and before 1964), have started to retire and will continue to do so over the next two decades. As they leave the workforce, they will leave a void that will result in a shortage of skilled labour in the Anglo-Saxon economies.
- The retiring baby boomers will put a huge burden on the economy as they will be spending money, i.e. drawing pensions from governments and corporations, as well as spending their own savings.
- Because of their large numbers as a percentage of the population, baby boomers will put huge strains on the current medical care system as they age.

These changes will be irreversible, at least for the 21st century. Change is always painful, particularly for those who are unprepared. By taking the initiative to read this book, you will be in a much better position to plan for the future.

'But where is the savings crisis in all this?' you may ask. The crisis stems from the simple fact that the 'system', i.e. governments, corporations, healthcare providers, pension schemes, etc., will not be able to handle such a demographic change in such a short (relatively speaking) period of time, and as a result it will fail at its weakest point, which we believe is likely to be in the area of pensions – our lifeline in

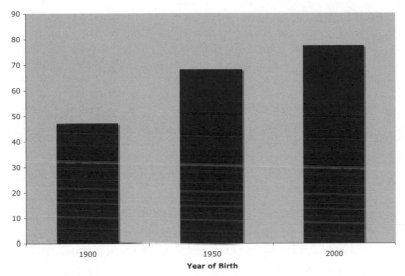

Life Expectancy Versus Year of Birth

Source: US National Center for Health Statistics. Other developed countries have very similar figures.

retirement. Unless we as individuals take steps to avert this future disaster, we risk living a miserably impoverished retirement, so we need to think wisely and make sure that we put enough away for retirement to ensure that this doesn't happen to us.

The vast majority of the populations in the Anglo-Saxon economies have not saved enough for their retirement. Most are still saving based on an era when life expectancy was less than 70, and without considering the unprecedented stress that the retiring baby boomers will be loading on the economy.

If you plan to retire on your state and/or corporate pension, you had better take a closer look at how much this will actually provide for you in retirement, as the vast majority of you will be shocked by how little you will have to live off once you have retired. To avoid disappointment and financial hardship in later life, make the time to really understand your financial position and follow our common sense advice.

Fast Facts

- *A boy born in the United Kingdom today has a 90 per cent chance of reaching the age of 65 and a girl has a 94 per cent chance.*

- *A boy born in the United Kingdom today has an 18 per cent chance of making it to 100 and a girl has a 24 per cent chance.*

- *If you are fortunate enough to make it to 65 (in the UK), your life expectancy actually goes up from 77.2 to 82.2 years for a man and from 81.5 to 84.9 years for a woman.*

- *The figures are similar for the United States – life expectancy at birth is 75.2 years for a man and 80.4 years for a woman. Again, if you're fortunate enough to make it to 65, your life expectancy goes up to 82.1 years for a man and 85 years for a woman.*

Governments have been too slow to react and haven't taken the bold and painful steps necessary to address the shortfall in state pension funds. Do you know what a full state pension is in the UK? It's £90.70[2] per week for a single person and £145.05[3] per week for a married couple. Annually, that's £4716.40 and £7542.60 respectively. Could you maintain your current lifestyle on this income, even if you had paid off your mortgage? Do not rely on the government to look after you in your retirement because it will be too busy raising taxes to make up the shortfall in tax revenue as a result of baby boomers dropping out of the workforce.

Governments will also be scrambling for additional income to fund the spiralling healthcare costs as a result of looking after the aging population. In short, governments will have their hands full

---

[2] Based on April 2008 rates.

[3] Based on April 2008 rates.

trying to make ends meet – don't expect any meaningful handouts from them by the time you retire.

Rather than spending sleepless nights trying to solve the governments' dilemma, it's more productive and valuable to think about your own predicament so that you won't have to hope that they will have figured everything out by the time you're a pensioner. It is our belief that they will not have. So be selfish and think about yourself and your loved ones because that's the only way to ensure your financial security. Ask yourself this alarming question:

How am I going to fund my life for 25 years without a salary?

Most of us can't survive more than six months without an income, let alone 300 months. If you think about how long 25 years actually is, you will appreciate how much money you will need to be financially secure for this length of time. Don't forget that you will end up spending more than you think in retirement, especially if you wish to maintain your lifestyle and enjoy privileges such as overseas travel. There will also be the high cost of medical care – especially private healthcare. Remember that as we get older, we don't have the luxury of time so we can't just put our names on a government hospital waiting list and hope we get a call in nine months, because it might be too late by then.

Getting older also means we're probably going to be popping a few life-extending pills (to combat diseases affecting our heart, cholesterol and blood pressure, to name just a few of the more common ones), as well as making the odd trip to the doctor and/or hospital.

To put some sort of perspective on this, most of us have a working life of around 40 years. In that time, we need to have saved enough for the next 25 years, so the stakes are very high. If we retire at 60, we have a good chance of making it to 90 and beyond. That's a long time to be living without a salary, wouldn't you agree? Will you have put away enough by the time you reach 60 or retirement age? Not knowing is the biggest danger because the last thing you want to discover is that you haven't saved enough for retirement after you have already retired. At that point it will be too late to do anything about it.

If that's not enough to concern you, we also believe that higher risk investments such as equities will experience increased uncertainty as a result of the retiring baby boomers. Why? Boomers' pensions will switch to lower-risk assets as they start to retire because they will need to draw on them regularly. As a result of the aging population, it is estimated that 20 per cent of the populations of the US and UK will be over 65 in the next 20 years. Think of all those investments currently in stocks today that will be switched to cash, bonds and other lower-risk assets. There will still be opportunities in equities as there have always been, but it will mean that picking the right stocks will be more crucial than ever.

Although this all sounds rather daunting, it need not be. Today, we have the luxury of two extremely precious resources that we can use to build wealth. The first is time, a truly invaluable commodity when seeking to build wealth. As obvious as it sounds, the second is a regular source of income, which for most of us comes in the form of a salary. Once we reach retirement, we lose both of these and it will by then be too late to do anything about changing our financial position (unless we win the lottery or inherit vast sums of money from a rich uncle we never knew we had – both extremely unlikely events, so don't gamble with your financial future).

Japan is a good leading indicator of what awaits many developed nations. Already, over 26 per cent of Japan's population is over 60 and its population as a whole is expected to shrink from its present 127 million to 100 million by 2050.

This spells disaster for the dependency ratio – a measure of the number of retirees/over-60s to the number of workers in a country. Countries with higher dependency ratios as a result of low birth rates and tighter immigration policies will no doubt undergo weaker economic growth and poorer investment returns.

The UN believes that, by 2020, the combined dependency ratio (over-60s to workers) of the US, Europe and Japan (these countries make up 70 per cent of the global economy) will shift from 30:70 to 50:50. Let's explain what this ratio shift is saying: today, there are 30 retirees/over-60s to every 70 workers; by 2020 they will be evenly matched, one-to-one.

Here is an example to illustrate the significance of this point: suppose that a retiree draws a pension of $100 per month. This $100 is collected in the form of national insurance/social security from the current workforce. For a dependency ratio of 30:70 (or 0.429), each worker would have to 'chip in' $42.90 in social security. Using the same example with a dependency ratio of 50:50 (or 1) means each worker's contribution would have to go up to $100 to ensure that a retiree can receive his pension. Granted, not everyone over 60 will be retired but the statistics are compelling nonetheless.

It is unlikely that workers' contributions will rise by the same amount to keep up with the rising dependency ratio without riots in the streets. So we believe that the most likely 'fix' will be a curbing of benefits to retirees, and a further raising of the retirement age, perhaps to around 72 years. Those dependent on the government for their pensions will be forced to work for a lot longer and get a lot less. That's just not an attractive future to look forward to.

We hope that by now we have been able to convince you of the magnitude of the situation and that as a result you are sufficiently motivated to act now by taking the right steps to secure your financial future before it's too late. We have written this book to share with you our *BigIdeas* for the coming decade which will ensure that you have invested wisely for your retirement.

In fact, these demographic changes lead us nicely into our first *BigIdea*. Although we haven't yet advised you on how to go about building wealth, this *BigIdea* is so closely linked with the aging population that we thought we would discuss it now while all the demographic facts are still fresh in your head. You will, of course, still need to read the 'how' later on in this chapter to fully appreciate how the big investment ideas fit into the overall picture of wealth creation.

BigIdea # 1

As you will have read earlier, or you may have known beforehand, we in the rich world are living longer. The global population is increasing (to 9 billion by 2050 from the current 6.7 billion), the percentage of people over 65 is also increasing (to 1 billion by 2030 from the current 500 million – doubling) and the baby boomers have started to get older and retire (right now, in the US alone, an average of 330 people are turning 60 every hour).

As an aside, there is a very interesting website that contains a world clock with a difference. This website tracks a multitude of statistics, including world population, births, population growth and deaths, to name just a few. It's worth spending a few minutes watching the rate that some of these numbers increase. The website is: www.poodwaddle.com/worldclock.swf.

Now, back to how we can turn an irreversible demographic trend into an investment opportunity. One of the ways this can be done is to invest in something that almost all old people use at some point in their life – no, not a golf course, something far less glamorous: nursing homes, sometimes referred to as assisted living. Some of the affluent retirees are opting for a more up-market environment by choosing to live in retirement communities instead. These allow retirees to still receive all the medical attention they need but without the dreary feeling of living in a hospital.

There is no doubt that we're going to need many more places where retirees can live, feel part of a community and have access to elderly care as and when needed. These retiring baby boomers are not going to hold back either – they will spend as much of their savings as it takes to ensure a comfortable retirement with 24/7 access to first class medical care.

So how do you go from identifying the concept of an investment opportunity to actually making an investment in this *BigIdea*? We're not suggesting that you go out there and start up your own nursing home, although if you have a business plan, the drive and the funding to do so, it could prove to be a very lucrative venture for you. Good luck. But for the rest of us who intend on keeping our day jobs, we suggest investing in a basket of companies that are well-established in this field and offer considerable growth opportunities.

There are quite a few companies out there that focus on building and/or managing homes for retirees. A few examples of such companies are Assisted Living Concepts (listed in the US), Brookdale (listed in the US) and Emeritus (listed in the US and Germany). If you have the time, the ability and the inclination, we would encourage you to do your own research in this field and invest in the companies you believe have the best growth potential.

We do, however, appreciate that you may not have the time, inclination or even the ability to analyze companies' financial data and make investment decisions based on your own analysis. But don't despair; it doesn't have to be that complicated if you don't want it to be. There is still an excellent investment opportunity for you in the form of a packaged, easy-to-buy financial product that invests in a basket of nursing homes/healthcare related companies. These packaged products are called REITs (Real Estate Investment Trusts) and there are quite a few REITs that specialize in this area. We discuss REITs in more detail in Chapter Three. There are around a dozen or so major REITs specializing in properties catering to retirees. Here are just a few to consider:

- Health Care REIT (ticker symbol: HCN). US-based, listed on NYSE. Founded in 1970, it was the first company to launch a REIT dedicated to healthcare properties. Website: www.hcreit.com

- Healthcare Realty (ticker symbol: HR). US-based, listed on NYSE. Founded in 1992, it specializes in medical office and out-patient facilities. Website: www.healthcarerealty.com
- Medical Properties Trust (ticker symbol: MPW). US-based, listed on NYSE. This company specializes in leasing state-of-the-art healthcare facilities. Website: www.medicalpropertiestrust.com

Get online, spend some time reading up about these REITs and pick the one you feel most comfortable with. Don't rush. This REIT will be part of your investment portfolio and integral to your wealth creation. If you really can't decide between two REITs, it is okay to choose both of them but we suggest you don't choose more than two. Incidentally, if you come across another healthcare REIT during your research, by all means include it in your short-list – the ones we name are just a few examples of the types of companies to invest in for this *BigIdea*.

BigIdea # 2

So compelling is the investment opportunity from the aging population that our second *BigIdea* also takes advantage of this trend. After all, the retiring baby boomer phenomenon is a sure thing and there aren't many of those around. The elderly will continue to make up an increasing percentage of the population and rich nations are faced with a record number of retirees on their hands.

So our second *BigIdea* relates to investing in companies that have the most to gain financially from serving or selling products and services to retirees and the older generation. Put yourself in a retiree's shoes – what would your needs be at that stage in your life, assuming that you've already found your nursing home or retirement community to live in? You'd be making sure that you had a good health insurance plan, that you took your medications regularly, and also your nutraceuticals, which are natural extracts that are believed to promote wellbeing and prevent certain diseases. An example of a common nutraceutical is glucosamine, which is taken in tablet form and used to maintain healthy joints and for the treatment of osteo-arthritis.

As unfortunate as it seems, we're also likely to be spending some time at doctors' clinics and possibly in hospitals, so we'll be using the latest screening techniques to diagnose our ailments as well as the next generation medical equipment – Magnetic Resonance Imaging (MRI) machines, ultrasounds and equipment that doesn't even exist today. Doctors may also be able to screen our DNA and determine what is wrong with us or what we are genetically predisposed to.

New breakthroughs and reduced costs will make cutting edge technology affordable to everyone. The types of companies that will likely be providing these products and services of the future are health insurance companies, pharmaceutical companies, companies specializing in research of one of more diseases – particularly the ones that tend to affect the older population, such as Alzheimer's – companies involved in genetic screening and sequencing, biotechnology companies, medical suppliers, and medical equipment companies. All of these can be categorized under healthcare.

We're not expecting you to analyze every company that falls under these categories, but we are trying to stimulate your thought processes because you may be developing your own *BigIdea* along these lines that we haven't mentioned so far.

For those of you looking for an easy-to-invest formula in health-care – and we're not saying that it's a bad thing – we recommend that you consider investing in a managed fund that specializes in healthcare. There are quite a few of these available today, each with its own angle. There are also Exchange Traded Funds (ETFs) to consider. These are passive funds that invest in a basket of listed companies. We explain more about ETFs in Chapter Four. Some

ETFs give a strong weighting to a handful of companies, whilst others cover around 30 companies. The latter would be less volatile as their performance won't hinge so much on the performance of a small basket of companies. Some ETFs have a very specific theme; others track one or more industries, regions, currencies, etc.

Let's discuss a particular ETF to give you a clearer understanding of what they are. We'll use a quite specialized healthcare ETF managed by iShares (part of Barclays PLC). The ETF is called Dow Jones U.S. Medical Devices Index Fund (ticker symbol: IHI) and invests in non-disposable medical equipment companies including manufacturers of medical devices, such as MRI scanners, prosthetics, pacemakers, X-ray machines and other non-disposable medical devices. At the time of researching this ETF, it was made up of a basket of 43 companies. To find out the names of these companies, you can go to the iShares website and look up this particular fund (www.ishares.com).

The important thing to remember here is the theme – medical devices. An aging population will increase the need for medical equipment, thus creating additional motivation for new and effective ways of diagnosing disease and prolonging life.

There are a number of other iShares healthcare ETFs you can look at in more detail, from healthcare providers to pharmaceuticals. If you can't decide on a specific healthcare theme, you can opt for the broader ETF entitled Dow Jones U.S. Healthcare Sector Index Fund (ticker symbol: IYH), but we like the more focused themes such as the medical devices, diagnostics or cancer research.

The Building Blocks to Prosperity

So what is the best way to go about planning the path to prosperity? After all, who wouldn't want to have a retirement that is free from financial concerns? Certainly, investing in some of our *BigIdeas* or some of your own *BigIdeas* will help in getting superior returns on your investment; however, fundamentally more important than that is building a stable financial footing from which you can invest and grow your wealth. We will refer to this as your investment platform.

In this section we discuss what we believe to be the building blocks of prosperity. Without these blocks in place, creating and building wealth becomes a serious uphill battle. We believe the building blocks to prosperity, in this order, are:

1 Eliminate Your Debts – the ones that charge the highest interest rates first
2 Live Within Your Means
3 Adopt the Discipline of Saving
4 Invest Wisely
5 Own the Home You Live In
6 Think Long-Term – the invisible block

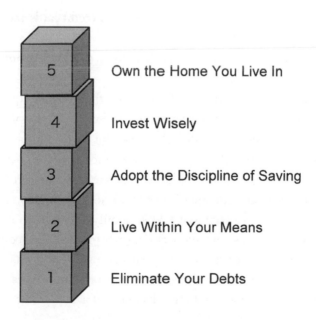

5 — Own the Home You Live In

4 — Invest Wisely

3 — Adopt the Discipline of Saving

2 — Live Within Your Means

1 — Eliminate Your Debts

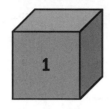

Building Block 1: Eliminate Your Debts

As we've stated many times before, especially in our previous book, *Wake Up!*, being in debt is the worst thing for creating wealth. The most dangerous of all debt is credit card debt. What is the point of trying to save money if you have an outstanding debt that is costing 20–30 per cent per annum to service? It's simply not possible to get a risk-free return on investment that is greater than the interest rate charged by credit card companies, so don't even try saving any money before you've paid off your debts.

Spend however long it takes as, without a doubt, this is the most important building block in wealth creation. Don't even try to move on to the next building block until you've eliminated your debts. This is the foundation block and if it's not in place, the stability of the other blocks is at risk. If your debt is scattered and out of control, consolidate it. Just remember these two guiding principles when it comes to debt consolidation:

1 The highest rate of interest is charged by credit cards and department store cards.
2 The lowest rate of interest is charged by mortgage lenders.

So take a moment to add up all your debt, then extract equity from your home mortgage (if you have one) and use it to pay off all your non-mortgage debt. You will feel a whole lot better for having done so, plus you will immediately save yourself money as the cost of servicing the debt will fall from an annual percentage rate (APR) of up to 30 per cent to around one fifth of this amount, which on a debt of $10,000 equates to a saving of $2400 in only one year. Think of this as a form of saving, as not paying this money to credit card companies as interest means it ends up in your pocket instead of theirs.

If you don't have a mortgage that you can tap into to release equity, consolidate your debt by taking advantage of a new credit card promotion that is offering debt consolidation and low to no interest for periods of three, six, or even nine months.

For readers living in the UK, it is worth visiting a comprehensive comparison site such as Moneyfacts (www.moneyfacts.co.uk) or Moneyextra (www.moneyextra.com) – you will be able to review the best credit card offers and the interest-free periods before deciding on the deal that is most suited to you.

Once you've consolidated your debt and you're living under the 'interest-free period' of the new card, you need to devote the bulk of your monthly wages towards paying off as much of your debt as possible. No expenses, other than essential commuting costs, groceries, rent and utility bills. Please don't dismiss this suggestion – it is simply a case of short-term pain for long-term gain.

Every month you remain in debt is another month in the opposite direction of saving and reaching your financial goals. The pain associated with adopting an aggressive debt repayment plan will also make you realize that credit cards are not a source of 'free money' and that this is literally pay-back for the months or years you have spent living beyond your means. Do it and kick the debt habit. Debt elimination is the start of wealth creation.

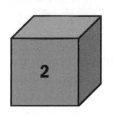

Building Block 2: Live Within Your Means

Putting it another way, living within your means is not spending more than you earn. For example, if your net income every month is $3000 after taxes, your total outgoings every month should not exceed this amount. As obvious as this sounds, the average household in most Anglo-Saxon countries is breaking this very basic rule every month, getting deeper and deeper into debt (see Building Block 1) and therefore preventing them from ever leaving Building Block 1.

Living within your means does not mean that you have to spend exactly what you earn either – you need to strike a balance so that you can meet your most essential financial obligations every month, such as food, rent/mortgage, medicines and transportation, and still have enough to invest. The amount that you need to put aside is very important and is determined by a number of factors that we shall cover towards the end of the book in Chapter Nine, on how to use our *DiagnosticGrid*.

After paying the bills, the mortgage and buying the groceries, many of us head out to the shops to spend the rest. This, unfortunately, leaves us cash-poor not long after payday and we end up having to hang on for the next pay-cheque to survive. Some impatient spenders may go one step further and resort to the dreaded credit card to buy things with money that they haven't even yet earned. It all starts off innocently and well-intentioned with a couple of impulsive purchases, but it doesn't take long before these purchases become compulsive. Buying on credit is, for many people, the start of a long, slippery slope into indebtedness that gets tougher and tougher to get out of.

This is clearly an unhealthy and unsustainable pattern. But old habits die hard and in order to realistically and successfully go about creating wealth we need to completely change our mindset about spending, investing and how we perceive debt. Getting stuck at Building Block 1 for a while is a result of not living within our means. If you qualified for Building Block 2 without having to stop at Building Block 1, congratulations, as Building Block 1 is the biggest of all hurdles. If you did spend some time on Building Block 1, then you will have more than learned your lesson on the consequences of careless spending and living beyond your means and you will certainly never want to revisit Building Block 1 again.

Having eliminated your debts (excluding the mortgage of your home), the next step is to rein in spending. In order to do this, you need to know what financial state you are currently in – if you think of your household as a small company, you need to look at its income statement; in other words, what are the household revenues or income, and what are its expenses? If revenues exceed expenses, then the household is making a 'profit', and this money can be 'reinvested' in the household's future, i.e. financial security through the creation of wealth.

If you would like some guidance on how to budget your household and how to classify each item of incoming or outgoing cash, we have prepared a simple budgeting template in Appendix A (p. 217), which can be used to get you going. Appendix A also contains a template to help you determine the current state of your finances – your household balance sheet. You can download a more comprehensive electronic version we have created called *DiagnosticGrid* by visiting www.bigideasbook.com and clicking on the Downloads tab.

Be honest in the budgeting process and don't forget to collect a receipt for the tiniest of purchases, as only then will you be able to discover where the 'leaks' in your wallet lie. At the end of the month you then need to take the pile of receipts and divide them into the following categories (as per the budgeting template in Appendix A):

1 Home (such as mortgage, rent, home repairs, bills, appliances and groceries)
2 Utilities (such as gas, telecom charges, electricity and water)
3 Transportation (such as car, taxi, train and bus)
4 Other (such as tuition fees, dental costs and medical bills)
5 Discretionary spending (yes, we need to include those shoes and handbags/purses because we know this is a soft spot for many ladies)

Once you've added up the spending in each of these categories, you will be able to clearly see (a) what you have left from your salary every month and (b) which categories are costing you the most.

Even if you don't manage to get a receipt for something, just put the amount and a brief description on a piece of paper and include it with the other receipts – otherwise you could be fooling yourself into thinking that the purchases that took place without a receipt won't impact the budget.

To really track your household finances, use your bank statements, your chequebook stubs and your credit card statements to complete the template, as this should provide you with all the information you need. If you are having trouble with this approach, try another: for an entire month, keep a receipt for every transaction you make. At the end of that month, you will be able to tangibly see what your money was spent on. Even the most disciplined are often surprised at how much money is 'wasted' on unnecessary expenses – dining out frequently and the liberal use of taxis (for the city dwellers) are two of the most common, but also it's those spontaneous retail therapy moments that give us the initial post-purchase euphoria before the item ends up being discarded and shelved for the remainder of its existence. Think before you buy. Ask yourself the following questions: How necessary is this item? How much utility will I get out of it? Is the price reasonable? Am I borrowing money (i.e. running a balance on my credit card) in order to afford it?

As a general guideline, we recommend that your household spending does not exceed 50 per cent of your net income – so that includes all items that fall under Home and Utilities in our budgeting template. If it does, it is more than likely you are living beyond your means and you need to make some adjustments before you are ready to embrace Building Block 3. Analyze your spending to identify where cost cuts can be made. It may simply be that you are living in a place that is too expensive for your current income level. If that's the case, don't be ashamed to move to a less expensive place. Remember that this would actually help you become financially better off so it would be a step towards creating wealth. See how your household spending is made up – are you spending more than 35 per cent of your net income on rent or mortgage payments? If so, you're probably living beyond your means as you won't have enough money left to allocate spending to the other categories and still be left with something to invest.

Although you are free to spend your money on anything you wish, we are fairly certain that you are reading this book because you are interested in learning how to save effectively and to build sustainable long-term wealth. Chances are that if you are currently living beyond your means, you either already know it or have a gut feeling telling you so (or a credit card balance that is keeping you awake at night).

Bear in mind that budgeting is not a science and every household is different, but at least this exercise will allow you to take a good hard stare in the mirror and understand how you are looking financially, as good or as bad as it may be. It will also allow you to see if your spending pattern is completely out of line with your income. This will force you to review each expense and determine whether you can reduce it or do without it altogether. For example, do you subscribe to any magazines that you don't read? Do you subscribe to a club that you rarely visit? Consider cancelling such subscriptions.

Once you've reviewed your spending and made the necessary adjustments (or even budget cuts), you should be left with some spare cash at the end of the month. If not, we're afraid that you are still living beyond your means and you will have to go back and make additional spending cuts. Only when you are able to come out with a surplus of around 10 per cent of your net income every month will you be ready for Building Block 3. The actual recommended percentage will be determined by our *DiagnosticGrid* in Chapter Nine, but 10 per cent is our broad guideline. Before moving on to Building Block 3, we need to ask you again, have you paid off all your debts (with the exception of the mortgage of your primary residence)? If not, you need to use your surplus money every month to pay off your debts, starting with the lenders that charge the highest interest rates. If you have any savings, the best use for them is to pay off your debts (excluding the mortgage of your primary residence).

Once you have done this, you are finally ready to start investing ...

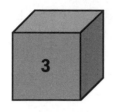

Building Block 3: Adopt the Discipline of Saving

Having cleared those burdensome debts and established a positive monthly cash flow, we can discuss how to go about building that nest egg. At the risk of sounding obvious, we believe the most effective way to build your wealth for later life is to invest a little amount on a monthly basis. Why monthly? Simply because most of us are paid monthly and it is the opportune time to invest some of our money before we are tempted to spend it foolishly on things that have no future value. If you are paid bi-weekly, investing monthly, i.e. every other pay day, would also work.

You need to change your mindset from spending what you earn – it's all about adopting a new and more productive habit of putting some money away every month from your salary or other income source. In time, this should become a habitual ritual, a life practice, drilled into your behaviour patterns until the day you are ready to retire.

You can view Building Block 3 as the transitional building block as it takes you out of the habit of living for today and towards one that prepares you for living for tomorrow. This doesn't mean that you'll have to stop living for today, of course, but it does mean that you'll need to give more thought to how you spend your hard-earned cash.

Remember that each month when we are paid is a unique opportunity for us to invest in our future prosperity and we should make the most of this opportunity. As tempting is it may be, don't yield to careless spending as you'll end up back at Building Blocks 1 and 2 for the rest of your life and with nothing when you retire. Stay in control of your finances, because if you're not in control of them, by default they are in control of you, and that is not a good position from which to become wealthy.

The unique *DiagnosticGrid* that we referred to earlier will help you to determine how much money you need to invest every month based on your current personal and financial circumstances. It will also help you with recommendations on how your investments should be allocated, i.e. what percentage should go into stocks, what percentage into currencies, gold, bonds, commodities, property, etc. So the output will be a tailored monthly investment plan to help you invest a little every month. This leads us nicely into our third big investment idea.

BigIdea # 3

To create a solid investment strategy that will withstand the test of time and provide you with some flexibility, we recommend that you structure your investments around your home, which should serve as your core asset. You can then allocate your investments around this based on the amount of funds you have available to invest. Once a structure that is suited to your financial profile has been created (and we help you with this in Chapter Nine, entitled DiagnosticGrid), you can then allocate the appropriate percentages every month based on the amount you have available to invest. The following diagram illustrates how an investment platform could look, where the home is the core asset.

The percentages shown above are indicative only and may not apply to your circumstances. You need to enter your details into the *DiagnosticGrid* to obtain your ideal percentage allocations.

Now you may be thinking that there is no way you can grow wealthy from putting away a few hundred dollars a month, so we will try to convince you with a couple of examples designed to show just how much of an impact compounded returns over time can have.

A 35-year-old person who manages to invest $500 (or pounds if you prefer) per month, with an average annual return of 5 per cent after tax on his investment, will be sitting on $77,641 in just ten years.

If you think that's impressive, let's introduce a third resource into the equation (the first two being money and time): wisdom – the great multiplier. If you took money, time and wisdom together and applied them to the same example above, the results would obviously be better. By investing wisely, you would be able to achieve a superior rate of return, say on average 10 per cent per annum after tax. After the same ten years, the same monthly investment plan would be worth $102,422, which is a 32 per cent better return on investment.

Now let's take this same example one step further to demonstrate what an incredible multiplier time and discipline can be.

If you followed the same investment plan of $500 per month from the age of 35 and were able to achieve an annual net return of 10 per cent for 20 years, at age 55 your nest egg would be worth a very respectable $379,684. This further illustrates that investing monthly is more effective and less burdensome than making lump sum investments. The other important point to emphasize is the way you invest your money really makes a difference over the years – as you can see, after 20 years of investing $500 every month, one can build a sizeable investment portfolio.

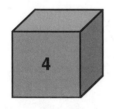

Building Block 4: Invest Wisely

Having created the right environment for your finances to flourish through the establishment of your investment platform, you are now ready for the important part – the investing. The reason

The Power of Compound Returns

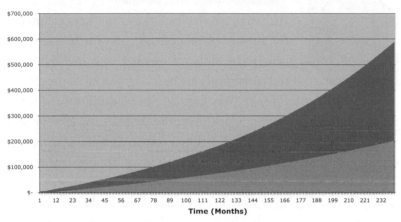

■ 5% Average Annual Return ■ 10% Average Annual Return

why this is so important in wealth creation is because investing wisely can mean the difference between an average annual return of 3 per cent versus 20 per cent. Compounded over 20 years, this makes a huge difference. For example, if we put $100 in an investment for 20 years earning 3 per cent per annum, at the end of that period it would be worth $180.61 – a growth factor of 1.8; but if that same $100 brought in an average annual return of 20 per cent, it would be worth $3833.76 over the same 20-year period – a growth factor of 38. So you can begin to see why investing wisely is such a valuable building block in allowing your money to work for you. Albert Einstein described compound returns as the 'eighth wonder of the world' and with the example above you can see why.

Much of our book is dedicated to investing in products and areas that we believe will provide you with superior returns on investment, but, again, these investments must be made from a stable platform over the long-term and diversified in a way to spread the risk and maximize the return. There are a number of asset classes available, each with their own pros and cons, and we discuss them separately in the subsequent chapters. But for the time being, let's move on to Building Block 5.

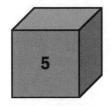

Building Block 5: Own the Home You Live In

Although we dedicate the entire next chapter to the subject of real estate, it is worth discussing briefly the value of owning your own home in the context of our building blocks to prosperity. Property has arguably been the hottest investment topic in the western world over the past decade. Everywhere you look, there's a frenzy of salivating investors and developers. And if that wasn't enough, there has been a barrage of property-related TV programmes, covering subjects such as fixing up homes, finding homes, selling homes, buying second homes, finding investment properties, etc. – you name it, chances are there's already a TV programme about it. This media exposure has certainly done its part in further feeding the property frenzy.

There is no denying that the past decade or so has seen some incredible increases in property prices. However, for the past few years we have been of the opinion that we were on borrowed time. In Britain, house prices rose by 205 per cent from 1997 to 2007, according to Nationwide Building Society. That's an annual average increase of 20.5 per cent. Sure enough, such levels of house price inflation proved to be unsustainable and prices in 2008 fell by 16% per cent from the previous year, with a general expectation that prices had a lot further to fall.

Over the same ten-year period, house prices in the United States increased by 175 per cent according to the Case-Shiller Home Price Index published by Standard and Poor's. That's an annual average increase of 17.5 per cent. They too of course have seen similar falls in 2008.

Wages have certainly not kept up with these increases. So how were people able to buy property at such stratospheric prices? Simple – by being offered incredible financing terms. The extra debt taken on didn't seem to bother home buyers because for some reason they had all got it into their heads that property prices would always go up, thus allowing them to make significant capital gains. This theory, of course, has proved to be nonsense.

Who could have imagined that it was possible to 'buy' a house without actually putting any money down and only paying off the interest of the loan every month? Does that really count as owning the house or is it simply holding the title to it on behalf of the bank/lender – the true owner of the house? It's really just a more elaborate and riskier way to rent.

With big falls in 2008, we don't expect prices to stabilize until two things happen: (1) banks start lending again; and (2) consumer confidence returns – without consumers believing that property prices have bottomed out, why would they even consider buying? By our reckoning, we don't believe these two things will happen until some time in 2010. Of course the global financial crisis could worsen further in 2009, which could push out the recovery to the tail end of 2010 or even 2011.

Now let's go back to the subject of owning the home you live in – when we say 'own', we mean a home you actually have some equity in. By that we recommend a minimum of 25 per cent and a partial repayment of the outstanding loan (principal) every month. If your stake in your home is less than 25 per cent, we suggest that you work towards increasing your home equity as a priority until you reach this target. If you own little to no equity in your home and 25 per cent seems like an unattainable target, we suggest you sell your home and rent a smaller place for a while until you have saved up enough for a 25 per cent down payment. The last thing you want to have happen to you is to get caught with only a 0–10 per cent equity stake in your home when property prices are nosediving. It would only take a 20 per cent drop in house prices, which has already happened in some regions, to send you into negative equity and then you're back to Building Block 1 and all the hard work of getting to Building Block 5 would be undone.

If you still think that there is some upside in the housing market and that you should hang on to your home and your nominal equity in it, then you're gambling with the future of your wealth. This book is about building wealth through long-term wise investments – leave the gambling to Las Vegas and Macau. If you've been caught out in the property crash and are now sitting on negative equity, try your best to renegotiate your mortgage with the bank. Try and get a deferral on your interest or principal repayments for a while. Banks are being more flexible during the credit crunch because the last thing they want is to repossess thousands of homes and to auction them off as a distressed asset. They stand to lose more than you and banks don't want to end up with a pile of repossessed homes on their books. They have enough problems as it is.

As a long-term goal, there is nothing like the feeling of owning your own home. The benefits are undeniable – the physical and mental security of having a roof over your head no matter what happens; the financial security of knowing that you could cash out if you wanted to or had to sell it, relocate, downsize, travel, etc. Let's not forget the significant increase in disposable income you would have – no longer would 25 per cent to 35 per cent of your salary disappear every month towards paying your mortgage or rent. This additional money could improve your lifestyle and allow you to strengthen Building Blocks 3 and 4.

Do not lose sight of the goal of owning your own home as the core building block in your investment portfolio. But don't rush to buy if the market is looking too expensive (like it is just about everywhere in 2008 and 2009) – property prices are cyclical. Be patient. Use the time to plan and save. Rent a humble place in the meantime to allow you to save more. We discuss real estate in more detail in the next chapter.

Pensions

Before moving on to the chapters that focus more on the types of investments you can make to build your investment portfolio, it is worth spending a few moments on a subject that is very important in countries with a relatively high tax base – pensions. The reason why it is important to factor pensions into your investment strategy is because of the tax breaks that are offered to investors by governments. For example, if you wanted to buy $1000 worth of a healthcare company, ideally you would try to do so from your gross income, i.e. before it has been taxed, otherwise you may need to earn, say, $1600 to net the $1000 after taxes. By investing within your pension scheme, your money would remain untaxed (although there are caps on how much you can invest) until you retire.

Seeing as you are investing largely for your retirement, you would not need to access this money until then in any case. Again, there are exceptions to when you can access your pension fund; the rules change frequently and are different for every country so you need to understand how it applies to where you live and work.

In order to ensure that you don't start drifting off, we'll only give you a brief outline of pensions, and we'll limit our scope to the UK, the US and Australia. Wherever you live, you need to speak with a pension specialist or financial advisor as he or she will be able to advise you of the most efficient way to invest in your *BigIdeas* to minimize your tax exposure. Pension laws and regulations are complex and in a constant state of flux, so it definitely pays to keep aware of these changes: not taking advantage of tax breaks in your country's pension schemes can drastically reduce the net amount of funds you use to make your investments. Also, investment gains made outside a pension scheme are often subject to other forms of tax, such as capital gains tax and dividends tax.

We hope we haven't started to lose you already ... have another shot of espresso and make sure that you at least understand the basics before you arrange to meet with a financial advisor.

In all fairness, we agree that it isn't the most riveting topic in the world because it forces us to think about retirement, which is associated with aging and edging closer to our inevitable departure from this world. But dying is unavoidable and an inevitable conclusion to living so we shouldn't delude ourselves into thinking that it somehow doesn't apply to us or that we won't get old – we will actually get older and live longer than ever before so we need to plan better for our retirement than previous generations. Not planning and preparing for our later life in advance will likely result in financial hardship and subsequent misery.

The best way to visualize how we should all be planning for our retirements is to think of ourselves as captains of big cruise ships at sea: it takes a lot of time to analyze our destinations, study the charts, chart the course and make subtle course adjustments along the way. We can't make drastic manoeuvres with a 100,000 tonne vessel, hence we need to know where we're going well in advance so we can pick the appropriate speeds and headings. We will certainly need to make course corrections along the way, but the further we drift from our heading the more drastic the course corrections will have to be. Similarly, the longer we leave the future of our finances unplanned, the more drastic the measures we will need to take to get us back on the right course. A well-planned trip with smooth sailing is our objective.

There are three sources of funds that can provide us with a pension when we retire: the government or state; our current or past employer(s); and ourselves (private).

State Pensions

Let us discuss state pensions first – and what a state they are in.

Given how we have already discussed the frightening rate at which the developed nations are aging, it will come as no surprise to many of you that almost all major developed nations are carrying massive pension liabilities – somewhere in the range of 100–250 per cent of Gross Domestic Product (GDP). Since governments of Western nations have already spent the pension contributions made by the generation of workers who are only now starting to retire, the burden falls on the current workforce to fund the pensions of these retirees – the baby boomers who have now started to retire and will continue to do so over the next 25 years. But the workforce over this same period will not be sufficient to provide pensions for these retirees.

In the UK, a fully paid-up worker, i.e. 44 years for men, 39 years for women, is eligible to receive a full state pension of £90.70 a week from the British government. That works out to be £4716.40 a year. So unless you're planning to retire in the remote fringes of the developing world or live like a hermit, grow your own vegetables and raise your own livestock, it isn't going to be enough money for you. This is the situation today. No doubt it will deteriorate further over the next 30 years. The state pension is so derisory that you are better off assuming that you will be receiving nothing from the state when you retire. It's best to view a state pension as a pleasant surprise should it still be around in some shape or form when you reach retirement age, but don't count on it in your retirement plans or you will surely be disappointed.

In the US, there is Social Security but it is in tatters. It is estimated that Social Security is under-funded by some $7 trillion and there does not appear to be a solution to address these unfunded liabilities. So, again, it is safe to assume that there will be no social security of any substance waiting for you when you retire. To make matters worse, the baby boomers are going to push the percentage of the population over 65 from 12 per cent to 20 per cent over the next 20 years. This will put further strain on social security.

Employer-Linked and Private Pensions

Many countries have a structured pension system that allows employees to put a percentage of their income away into a pension fund every month during their working life. The tax breaks tend to be attractive enough to make investing in this way worthwhile. The problem is that not many people know how their money is working for them while they dutifully say goodbye to a chunk of their pay cheque every month, because many pension schemes are not very transparent. In addition to that, investors seldom take an active role in managing their pension funds.

The UK

UK residents are rather fortunate when it comes to non-state pensions – it has very generous tax breaks and legislation that favours the employee, yet many of us are not taking full advantage of them. As we have already explained, we completely advise against anyone relying on a state pension for retirement as it will not be enough to live off and in all likelihood will not even be around by the time most of the post-baby boomer generation (often referred to as generation X) retires.

Most employees are enrolled in a company pension scheme of which there are two types: a defined contribution scheme and a defined benefit scheme.

A defined contribution scheme is essentially a segregated account set up specifically for your pension, which you and the employer invest into. The employer is not responsible for the pension's performance and whatever it is worth by the time you retire is yours to keep (provided you have worked with the employer long enough to have the right to the employer contributions).

A defined benefit scheme is when an employer guarantees an employee a percentage of his or her salary upon retirement for the rest of his or her life. Typically, employees with 40 years of service would receive two-thirds of their salary at the time of retirement for the rest of their lives. Whilst this is an excellent arrangement for long-serving employees, it is an incredible headache for companies offering this annuity pension to its employees. They need to determine the demographic profile of their work force and employ expensive actuaries to advise them on how much cash they need to free up from their balance sheets to make these pension payments.

Pension liabilities can run into the billions of pounds for large corporations. A few of the companies with the largest pension liabilities on the London Stock Exchange are BT (£39 billion), Royal Dutch Shell (£31 billion) and Royal Bank of Scotland (£27 billion).

It is no wonder that companies are doing everything they can to switch over to the defined contribution scheme. If you are fortunate enough to be enrolled in a defined benefit pension scheme, do everything you can to hang onto it. It's a benefit that truly outweighs any other and is being phased out so don't let it go without a fight. It is also worth putting in the years of service required to ensure a guaranteed salary during your retirement. However, there is no sure thing in this world and you are exposed to the risk, however remote, of your employer going bankrupt at any time between now and the day you depart from the land of the living. That could be 25 years from now or 55 years from now – either way, it's a long time and anything can happen, even to today's FTSE powerhouses. Many of today's big corporations were not in the same position 30 years ago.

The government has taken some steps to address this risk to employees and retirees: in 2005, it established the Pension Protection Fund (PPF) to ensure that retirees continue to receive their pension in the event the employer goes bust. The catch is that there's a cap on the amount the PPF commits to covering if your employer goes bust before you retire. At the age of 65, this cap was £30,856.35 for the 2008–2009 tax year, so if your pension is likely to be more than this amount, then you are still exposed to the possibility of your employer going bust at some point between now and when you retire.

Although there isn't much you can do to ensure the future survival of your employer (unless of course you are the Managing Director/ CEO of your company, in which case you're at the helm), we recommend that you keep an eye on any changes that are being considered to the company pension scheme. If you are ever offered a lump sum cash payment instead of a guaranteed salary during retirement (annuity), consider it carefully. A lump sum payment means you are no longer exposed to your company's success in the future and the money would be transferred to your name to invest and to live off directly. We are the type of people who prefer to have our money under our control, so we would opt for taking the lump sum pension payment if it were ever offered to us – provided it was a fair amount, of course.

If you are enrolled in a defined contribution pension scheme with your employer, it can be either contributory or non-contributory in nature. The contributory scheme means that you are required to invest a portion of your gross salary (usually 5 per cent) towards your pension, whereas the non-contributory scheme means that the employer is making all the pension contribution each month.

Quite often in the contributory scheme, the employer will match or sometimes even double the employee's contribution. So, for example, if you put away £200 per month towards your pension (which is not taxable), your employer would also contribute £200 or even £400 per month in addition to your contribution, which means that you have immediately doubled or even trebled your pension investment amount before your money has started to work for you. And did we mention that it's tax-free?

The downside of a defined contribution scheme (both types) is that in many cases employees don't have many investment choices or much flexibility in the products available to them.

If you work for a smaller company and your employer does not have a pension scheme set up, we recommend that you consider setting up a personal pension to take advantage of the tax relief. A Self-Invested Personal Pension (SIPP) allows investors to have reasonable control of how their money is invested and also offers a broader range of products, including:

- Shares
- Cash deposits
- Insurance company funds
- Bonds
- Commercial property and land
- Unit trusts and investment trusts
- Futures, and
- Options.

This would allow our UK readers to invest in our (or your) *BigIdeas* in a tax-efficient manner.

For more information on UK pensions, read through the FAQ section at the HM Revenue and Customs website: http://www.hmrc. gov.uk/pensionschemes/faqs/contoccs.htm#a

We should also mention another vehicle available to UK residents that is exempt from taxation – Individual Savings Accounts, or ISAs, as they are more commonly known. There are no restrictions on having an ISA and a private pension at the same time. The main difference between an ISA and a pension is that you make your payments into an ISA from your NET income, i.e. income that you've already been taxed on. But once the money is in the ISA, it is exempt from income tax and capital gains tax.

ISAs are very flexible and can be used to invest in most asset classes in any geography. Upon retirement, the ISA can be converted into an annuity (an ongoing income, often monthly). ISAs come in two flavours: a maxi-ISA and a mini-ISA.

The investment limits of ISAs are set by the government and are subject to change, but at the time of writing, you could invest up to £7200 a year in a maxi-ISA (using one ISA investment manager), or you could invest into a number of mini-ISAs, each under a different asset class and different investment manager. So you could set up a number of mini-ISAs; for example, one in cash and another in stocks and shares. There is also a limit under each mini-ISA which is determined by the asset class of the mini-ISA. It is also worth mentioning that you cannot have both types of ISA at the same time, so it's best to discuss ISAs with a financial advisor to determine whether they are a good fit with your *BigIdea* investment plans.

The US

In the US, there is the 401(k), an employer-sponsored retirement savings plan. In many cases, the employer also contributes to the employee's plan, sometimes 50 per cent of the employer's contribution, sometimes matching it. The reason why they are attractive to employees is because 401(k) plan contributions are made from the gross salary, i.e. pre-tax. As long as the funds remain within the

401(k), they are exempt from tax. To some extent 401(k) plans offer the flexibility of being self-directed and portable.

If you don't have an employer-sponsored plan such as a 401(k), you can consider setting up what's referred to as a Roth IRA (Individual Retirement Account). This is widely considered to be the most advantageous retirement scheme available after an employer-sponsored retirement plan such as a 401(k). One drawback to it, though, if you want to be an aggressive saver, is that it has a contribution limit of only $4000 per year (this amount may have changed by the time you read this book).

We're almost there, just one other thing to add ... in 2006, the government introduced a new investment scheme called a Roth 401(k), which combines the features of the traditional 401(k) with those of the Roth IRA.

It is offered by employers just like a 401(k) plan, but the Roth IRA contributions are made with after-tax dollars. However, once the money is in the Roth IRA, it can grow tax-free. Additionally, any withdrawals made during retirement will not be subject to income tax (as long as you're at least 59½ years old and you've had the account for at least five years). The contribution limit for the Roth IRA is around $15,000 but you'll need to check that as these limits tend to be adjusted every now and then.

Basically, the difference between a 401(k) plan and a Roth IRA plan is down to when the tax is paid: with a 401(k) the money is not taxed on the way in, but is on the way out; with a Roth IRA, after-tax money goes in, which is then typically tax-free coming out.

Australia

In Australia, the mandatory retirement investment vehicle is known as a superannuation, often just referred to as a 'super'. All employers are required to enrol their employees into a super and must contribute a minimum of 9 per cent (there is a cap on the amount) of the employee's base salary into a super fund of the employee's choice. Employees have the option of topping up their super by making contributions from their gross salary.

Since its introduction in 1992, the superannuation pension scheme has been working well in establishing a financial safety net for retirees. By the end of 2007, total superannuation assets were around $1 trillion (Australian dollars) and are forecast to reach $2 trillion by 2014. For many people, their superannuation ends up being their most significant asset by the time they retire.

The super can also include components of life insurance cover and disability insurance. Given the high tax base in Australia, we recommend that you contribute as much of your income as is permissible into your super fund to minimize your tax exposure.

Chapter *Three*

Real Estate

Real estate, bricks and mortar, property – whatever you want to call it – is the most emotive of all investment classes. Because we all need shelter and have a compelling desire to 'own' the home we live in, quite often real estate is approached in a less than dispassionate way.

Our view of property in the next ten years is largely coloured by the geographical location of our readers. The old adage about real estate that it is all about 'location, location, location' has never been more applicable than today – but in a different sense.

Today, a careful MACRO view of global property location is required.

When we first published this book in early 2008, our advice was for everyone to avoid all types of property in Anglo-Saxon markets as well as those in Australia, New Zealand, Eastern Europe and most of the rest of Europe. We were also ambivalent about buying property in India and China.

Today, property in all of the key markets we discouraged readers from investing in is down by at least 20 per cent and in some of them by a lot more. The only exception is Germany, which was and remains our top tip for residential property, where by most estimates property prices have RISEN since this book was first published.

In a nutshell, we think that the overheated Anglo-Saxon property markets are way past the peak of their cycles, and are likely to remain in a bear or down phase until early 2010 or so. These markets, broadly encompassing the United States, Australia, New Zealand, Ireland and the United Kingdom, have experienced phenomenal real price inflation in property over the past ten years, despite the recent price falls.

In the first edition of our book, we wrote:

'There are strong reasons to suppose that those good days are drawing to a close and that potential buyers should be wary about buying incremental real estate of *almost any type* in those particular countries.'

But we also tempered that advice by recognizing that many of our readers own the homes they live in, possibly with the help of a mortgage. It is unrealistic of us to expect that, based on our recommendation, people would sell their homes and move into rented accommodation in order to take advantage of a down cycle.

The disruptive effects of moving for a possible economic gain are just too great for most people, so we recognized that a 'sell' recommendation on property in the above-mentioned countries would have limited resonance. That is, except to those who were contemplating buying incremental or investment property. Or indeed, to those who were thinking of putting themselves onto the so-called 'property ladder' for the first time.

Nonetheless, we believed there were compelling reasons for supposing that certain overheated property markets were nearing their peaks and that, in broad terms, new investment should be avoided. These did not only include the Anglo-Saxon economies but also other real-estate markets where feverish speculation had been a hallmark of recent activity. For instance, Spain, France and some of the Nordic European countries fell into this category.

In all of these, we suggested extreme buyers' caution.

Today, our advice is somewhat different. In fact, it's very different.

Property is an important part of everyone's portfolio and long-term wealth creation, and at some point it will clearly become a good buy again. Nothing goes down for ever – the trick is to find the inflection point, or at least approximately so.

In some markets that inflection point is being reached, and in others it will be reached soon.

We believe that German residential property remains an excellent buy, and we continue to strongly promote its inclusion in a balanced portfolio.

In the United States and in the United Kingdom, readers should be prepared to buy property some time in early 2010, which is when we expect the market to stabilize.

Our prediction is based on three important factors:

1 The injection of huge amounts of liquidity in both the US and in the UK will begin to have an effect on bank lending, and by 2010 – or perhaps slightly before then – there should be the beginnings of a resumption of confidence amongst consumers and homeowners.

2 Prices will have fallen further by then. In the first publication of this book we thought that Anglo-Saxon housing markets would fall by 40–50 per cent from peak to trough. There is always a lag in official figures, and we now estimate that over three quarters of the falls have taken place in many areas. Therefore at some stage in the next few months, investors should be looking to put in 'cheeky' bids on properties in the US and the UK, especially in foreclosure sales, and from developers who are anxious to sell newly built properties in order to straighten out their balance sheets.

3 The supply of properties remains highly constrained in the UK, and demographic factors remain positive. In the US, the inventory of unsold homes remains high, but with mortgage applications on the rise, that inventory could be reduced quite quickly. This is especially so if inflationary expectations start to creep in early 2010, as we expect. This means that in most areas, US house prices should reach a bottom towards the end of 2009.

The prospects for a fast upturn are good in both countries simply because property remains the best inflation hedge. It has the characteristic of being leveraged (i.e. debt-financed), so that as inflation rises the value of the debt (providing it is fixed at constant rates for a long period) diminishes, and the value of the property goes up.

Because we believe that the United States is DELIBERATELY laying the foundations for high inflation in order to reduce the size of the government's future debt burden, the effects of this will be highly positive for property. But in order that your monthly mortgage payments don't skyrocket once inflation starts to pick up and central banks raise lending rates, make sure you secure a LONG-TERM FIXED RATE MORTGAGE. That way, once rates start going up in an effort to put the brakes on inflation (and we believe rates may go up substantially), you will have the comfort of knowing that the interest rate on your mortgage will not be affected.

Unlike in Japan or in Germany, where property prices have stagnated for nearly 20 years, we see a big upturn in UK and US property prices ON THE BACK OF INFLATION AND RESUMED BANK LENDING – starting sometime in 2011.

Our view is that investors should therefore look at the following:

1 German residential property remains our favourite investment, and the best ways to invest in it are through well-managed funds specialising in that field.

2 UK residential property prices will bottom about 40 per cent below their peak sometime in late 2009/early 2010. This will present an excellent buying opportunity for investors. We would recommend at that stage buying inner city new build developments from foreclosure sales, in cities such as London and Birmingham. We also think there will be good value in certain commercial property where it is rented to long-term, good quality tenants at upwards-only rentals.

We do not think that the Irish, Australian, New Zealand or Eastern European property markets will represent good value for several years to come. They are all overbuilt and the vacancy levels remain – and will continue to remain – high.

We reiterate our fundamental advice, that it *is* a good idea, in our opinion, no matter where you live, to ultimately own your own property. It *is* a good strategy for investors to look beyond their own borders at property investments overseas, and it *is* a good idea to look at proxies for direct property investment. These can include real estate investment trusts (so-called REITs); mutual funds investing in property; property companies listed on stock markets; and a variety of other surrogate property investments.

This chapter is going to propose the following:

1 If you live in an Anglo-Saxon economy and do not possess unlimited financial resources, don't buy additional property until prices have fallen by at least 40 per cent from their peak levels. We thought this would take ten years from the book's initial publication but now we believe that the buying opportunity will appear sooner, at least for UK and US investors.

2 If you live in Spain, and possibly France and certain Nordic and Baltic countries, you should continue to avoid property, probably for some years to come. China, Singapore, Hong Kong and other Asian markets – especially India – may have overheated, but will probably remain relatively stable, albeit volatile, over the next ten years. This is because of limitations on available space, newly aspirant middle classes in the case of China and India, and an already considerable shakeout in prices.

3 For the more mobile or adventurous home owner, we recommend that you sell and rent while prices drift down. In almost all of these markets, the effective net rental yield (the amount that a landlord receives net for renting out a property) was below the net cost of capital. In other words, the days when a mortgage could be paid out of rental income with surplus to spare were

truly over in many markets. In some cases, however, the scale of the price falls has been so large that this may no longer apply and as a result investors there should start thinking in 'buying mode' again.

4 If you are a first-time buyer considering taking on a big mortgage relative to your income, we repeat what we said in the first edition of this book: 'Have a cold shower, take a walk and DON'T DO IT. In our strong opinion you will be able to buy your own place more cheaply in five or ten years' time if you live in the UK, US or almost all of the other overheated/ing countries we have mentioned. In the meantime, rent.' Even we, pessimistic as we were, didn't think that the price falls we contemplated would be concentrated in just two years. Now that advice is turned on its head – the 'Great Correction' (as we term the current period) will be over rather faster than most expect so investors should start preparing to BUY. Mind you, that advice only applies to the selected markets we discussed. Also, if you plan on getting a mortgage, it is very important that you secure a LONG-TERM FIXED RATE mortgage.

5 If you own your own home, but have plenty of equity in it, are happy there and have spare cash to pursue some of the other investment strategies, we recommend that you stay where you are. Although property prices are likely to fall a bit further, you don't need the money or the hassle. Besides, you're probably too set in your ways to live in rented accommodation. But one thing you should not do – and reverse out if you have – is to buy additional property until prices fall to our target levels in the markets we recommended.

Since we believe that inflation will be resurgent sometime in late 2010, and because it takes longer to buy property than, say, stocks and shares, and because investors will want to arrange FIXED RATE mortgages on their property investments, we suggest that preparations are set in motion soon. A fixed rate mortgage will lock-in the monthly repayments no matter how high interest rates get to, and this point is key in allowing investors to benefit from rising property prices without the risk of being burdened with higher mortgage rates.

So to recap: we believe that everyone should seek to own the home they live in – in the long-term. Jumping onto the property bandwagon without careful thought is a foolish leap to potential penury.

Because real estate is one of the few areas of investment where 'gearing' (i.e. taking on debt) is a possibility for individuals, it has a seductive charm of its own. When it is going up, the returns on 'equity' (the amount of the value of the home minus the debt) can be spectacular.

For instance, if Ms X buys a one million dollar (US) home, and puts $100,000 down (and for the sake of simplicity we will omit those irritating variables such as transaction costs and taxes), and then the price of her home goes to $1.5 million, what happens?

Well, her 'cost' is $1m, deductible from the sale value of the home, of $1.5m. A profit of $500,000 on an investment of just $100,000 – a fivefold increase. Beat that, Ms X might say.

'Gearing', or 'leverage', in the form of mortgage or other real estate debt really comes into its own in a rising market. Yes, interest has to be paid on the debt, but generally, in a real estate bull market, that particular cost is outweighed many times by capital appreciation.

It's for that reason that real estate, fuelled by massive amounts of mortgage debt, has been such a winning investment in Anglo-Saxon and other economies in the past two decades and why early-birds (generally people over 50 in those countries) ended up with by far the largest part of national wealth. In the UK, property was estimated to account for over 60 per cent of national wealth at its peak in 2008.

This is because – generally speaking – the older generations have been accumulating the largest portion of real estate at the lowest (i.e. earliest) prices, and have had longer to accumulate it and to pay off the debt associated with their original investment. They have also had the advantage of living in this real estate effectively for free.

So it's not surprising that the next generation took it as a given that the price of real estate can only rise and that they too should jump on the bandwagon.

Since an entire industry – the mortgage lending industry – grew fat and happy lending to people on ever-rising house prices and that industry enjoyed very low 'default' or 'delinquency' rates, credit in most Anglo-Saxon economies and in countries such as Spain was very easy to acquire for new buyers until the 'Great Correction' started in mid-2008.

But the people who took on debt of alarming magnitude, at unsustainably high rates of payments relative to their incomes, and who bought property at very high prices that have gone down considerably, are now regretting their actions, to say the least. These people were also taking out mortgages of increasing duration, i.e. ones that take many more years to pay off – quite often with 'teaser' terms that made it easier to pay in the early years but become much more onerous later on.

Now let's return to our Ms X example to illustrate the consequences of gearing in a falling market.

Let's suppose that our mythical Ms X sells her house for $1.5 million and that the new buyer, Mr Y, puts down 10 per cent of the 'new' value of the home, i.e. $150,000.

In two years' time, Mr Y has to sell his house (perhaps he has lost his job, or the interest payments have become too much for him, or he has to move for another reason). Unfortunately, there has been a sharp fall in real estate prices over the period, so Mr Y can only sell the house for $1.3 million (net of all costs). That means he has sustained a loss of $200,000. What are the effects of this loss? Well for a start he would have lost his $150,000. It would be gone, never to be returned.

Second, there is deficiency on his sale price relative to the debt ($1.5 million minus his original $150,000 = $1.35 million). He still owes the bank $50,000.

Nasty. But surely he can just walk away from that debt, having sold his house? No – generally speaking, he can't. Most mortgages are recourse ones – in other words, you put up a personal guarantee so that if you can't discharge the entirety of the mortgage you STILL owe the bank or lending institution – even if you have SOLD the property. This personal guarantee is rarely enforced in most US states but it most certainly is in the UK.

So, our mythical Mr Y remains in hock to the bank for $50,000 – which he either pays, or goes into bankruptcy over the debt. Not a pleasant situation to be in.

But surely, you might say, Mr Y has avoided paying rent for those two years and that will have saved him some money.

Sure – but remember Mr Y has lost $200,000 altogether – the entirety of his equity plus another $50,000 that he owes to the bank – and will continue owing to the bank until he pays it off.

He will also have had to pay all sorts of fees in terms of buying and selling his property, but we will leave those to one side for the sake of this argument.

One thing we cannot ignore is the interest he will have paid the bank on his mortgage debt over the period. Let's put that at 6 per cent per annum. On a debt of $1.35 million that's $81,000 per annum (substitute any currency for this example – it works in all of them).

In addition, he might have had to pay what is called 'amortization' or principal repayments – in other words, the portion of the debt that you are obliged to pay back every year to the bank, but to mitigate the pain of this example still further, we will avoid that for the moment.

In some countries, interest is partly tax-deductible, so there may be an offsetting benefit for Mr Y, but we will ignore that to even up the scales slightly.

So in summary:

- Mr Y is down $200,000 from the sale of his house.
- He has had to pay $81,000 × 2 in interest charges for the two years he has been living there.

- There are other costs which will almost certainly outweigh any tax advantages for him but we will ignore them for the sake of simplicity.

That's a grand total loss of $362,000.

He has of course saved on rent – but how much?

Well, in Anglo-Saxon economies, the general rental yield had by 2007 fallen BELOW the cost of capital. In other words it cost more to borrow than the generally available rental yield (rental yield being rent received expressed as a percentage of the value of the house).

If Mr Y had rented a house comparable to the one he paid $1.5 million for, it would have cost him four per cent of $1.5 million per annum.

That's $60,000 per annum.

Or a total of $120,000 over two years.

Offsetting that, of course, is the fact that he would have received INCOME (let's say at four per cent net) on his $150,000 deposit that he never had to use. That's a total of $12,000 over two years.

We hope you are following us because this is **IMPORTANT** – we are demonstrating the perils of a misguided over-enthusiasm for real estate. And many millions joined in this lemming-like rush to invest in property right at the top.

So overall, Mr Y lost $362,000 by buying a property at the wrong price and selling it two years later. He has saved rent of $120,000, but has foregone interest income of $12,000 that he could have earned by depositing the $150,000 in the bank for two years at four per cent interest, instead of using it as a down-payment.

His total loss is therefore $254,000 – on equity of $150,000 that's pretty horrendous.

Now just imagine that the same facts and rough and ready arithmetic prevail but that instead of selling for $1.3 million, Mr Y has to sell for $1 million. This is entirely conceivable, given the collapse in Anglo-Saxon prices that has occurred in recent months.

After all, it wasn't that long ago that Ms X BOUGHT the property at that price. It's very likely that it could go back to that original price.

In those circumstances – trust us, we've done the maths – Mr Y would be down not $254,000 net on his 'investment' but $554,000 – a really horrendous outcome.

That's the downside of real estate investment – and it's one that should by now be ringing in people's heads in the Anglo-Saxon and Spanish economies in particular.

Yes, we know we can't time these things perfectly, but what buyers in these countries did in 2007/2008 was to engage in a late-stage pass-the-parcel game where there weren't many winners.

Let us explain why.

The factors that drive real estate are numerous but the key ones in our opinion are:

1 **The macroeconomic cycle**. That is, key economic indicators such as GNP growth, interest rates and the levels of employment in an economy.

2 **The cost-of-replacement factor**. If real estate is relatively cheap to build compared to its final price, then given that there is land to build on (and in some cases we recognize that that is a big 'if'), then the price of real estate will gradually fall to its replacement cost as more of it is produced.

3 **The affordability factor**. This is broadly defined as the amount of debt that an individual can 'afford' to take on in relation to his or her salary. It is normally expressed as a multiple of income – in other words Ms X can 'afford' to take on three times her salary in debt. In recent years, Anglo-Saxon banks have been arranging for this multiple to expand to unprecedented and, in our view, unsustainable levels.

4 **The locational aspect**. Of course, within countries, there are differences, and often great ones, between real estate prices – so LOCATION will make a big difference to prices both up

and down. Two examples: first, London in the UK, which has amongst the highest real estate prices in the world. This is partly because of London's new role as the world's financial capital and the influx of wealthy foreigners attracted to the UK's benign tax regime for foreigners. This influence supercharged London property prices until mid-2008. A second example is Las Vegas in the United States, for years the best performing real estate market in the country but which in 2006 went into sudden reversal. Excessive speculation caused a bubble and eventually the bubble burst.

So, let's analyze each one of these factors in relation to the markets that went DOWN, in accordance with our forecasts made in the first edition of this book in early 2008.

In broad terms, the outlook for the major Anglo-Saxon economies went from being benign to being extremely difficult. Interest rates first trended upwards as a result of inflationary pressures, partly caused by excessive levels of debt and consumption, and by heavy government borrowing. Rising interest rates, which are normally a warning sign for real estate markets, should have been a clear signal to investors since interest payments on mortgages and other types of real estate debt become more onerous as rates rise. These interest rates have now gone into rapid reversal in the Anglo-Saxon economies as governments have attempted to unfreeze the credit markets.

Growth levels for Anglo-Saxon economies have come to a shuddering halt and most of them are expected to be in severe recession in 2009 and possibly beyond. Hardly an inspiring backdrop for real estate.

The United States is now suffering the consequences of an excessively easy monetary policy, i.e. too much credit had been created and at the same time the country had a very negative trade imbalance. This led to a weakening dollar up to the first half of 2008, which was bad for inflation, as the cost of buying goods from overseas became higher for Americans with their weakened dollars.

In order to stem inflation, the Federal Reserve, the Central Bank of the United States, had to adopt a 'tightening' stance with regard to the creation of new credit. This started aroun the end of 2007, and the tightening process indirectly led to the many failures of financial firms and others which we have seen since.

Real estate markets feed on credit and in recent years a whole new sub-class (but accounting for up to 20 per cent of total US mortgage lending) of real estate lending – the now notorious 'sub-prime' mortgage market emerged. Sub-prime lending, which is now history, was where lending institutions (some of them now near or in bankruptcy), specialized in lending to just about anyone who wanted to buy real estate. Discharged bankrupts, people with no or poor credit history – you name it, they took them on.

And how they reaped the whirlwind.

When real estate prices in the more speculative markets in the United States, such as Florida, Las Vegas, and Phoenix, etc., started to falter, there was a rush to the doors, as many of those gambling with borrowed money tried to cash in their chips. For quite a few, there was no market to sell into and because the sub-prime lenders weren't getting their interest payments covered by their 'distressed' borrowers, they started to 'foreclose' on their loans.

This was the earliest manifestation of distress in what was formerly a superheated US real estate market.

In the year before, 2005, the beginnings of a downturn occurred in Australia, a country for years in thrall to real estate madness. Overbuilding of 'buy to let' (or rental) properties in the key Sydney, Melbourne and Brisbane markets was a harbinger of downturns to come.

In the United Kingdom, real estate prices at the beginning of 2007 displayed, for the first time for at least a decade, some patchy evidence of softness. The Bank of England was at that time raising interest rates to avert inflationary pressures and every ratchet upwards put a little bit more pressure on the clearly overheated property market.

In Spain, which was the subject of almost rampant real estate speculation – to the extent that the property and construction sectors accounted for 18 per cent of the total economy at its peak – 2007/8 saw near total collapse in certain real estate sectors. Spain became so overbuilt that this is one market which will possibly take a decade or more to recover.

None of this is surprising when one considers the ferocity and longevity of the bull markets in real estate in these countries. Fuelled by easy money and by the promise of easy profits – with debt accessible to almost any sentient being – the mania became pervasive. In fact, in Ireland real estate became so ingrained in the national psyche that property prices seemed to occupy the bulk of almost any conversation up to the dying days of 2008.

What amazed us as authors was that, despite all the evidence pointing to a massive correction in real estate prices, most people buried their heads in the sand. The obvious question was of course:

When everyone appears to be on the bandwagon, who is left to buy property?

Only those who could not really afford the leap onto the property ladder, or whose poor financial standing could be undone by a number of adverse factors – rising interest rates (more expensive mortgages), declining employment (more people out of work), or the 'madness of crowds' in reverse (many people trying to sell into weakening markets at the same time).

In almost all of the Anglo-Saxon economies, affordability ratios were stretched to breaking point, property sold at a very high multiple of its replacement cost and macroeconomic factors were becoming less benign. Furthermore, a large number of people had increased exposure to the property market over and above their own home ownership. The buy-to-let mania in the UK was one example, where stories abound of individuals sitting on top of large rental portfolios almost entirely financed by bank debt and by hope. Hope will now spring eternal for most of them.

Speculative 'off-the-plan' investments in the US, Spain and Ireland were also very popular at that time. This is where developers 'pre-sold' properties not yet built from 'plans'. Put a deposit down now, is the idea, and the price will be much higher when the property is completed, or so the implied promise went. You can then pay the rest and garner your profit.

Or perhaps not. Because if by then prices have gone down, and you are committed to paying a high price for a development which is to be completed sometime in the future, you have two options:

One is to walk away from your deposit, and to lose what is typically 10 to 25 per cent of the final price of the completed property.

The second is to pay up and sit on a loss. Possibly for many, many years.

Neither option is a particularly attractive proposition.

All these factors (summarized below) and more make us wary of the big Anglo-Saxon (which, by the way, excludes Germany) real estate markets:

1 Macroeconomic factors are not as benign as they had been.
2 Affordability indicators are stretched to breaking point.
3 Locational factors not as important as they once were – the old adage that a rising tide floats all ships applies to real estate as well.
4 Almost every area of property opportunity has been uncovered in Anglo-Saxon markets and just about every area has had its own mini property boom. There aren't really any localized 'bargains' to be had any more.
5 The first cracks – sub-prime mortgage distress in the US, weakening price momentum in the UK and in Ireland, downright panic in Spain, and persistent weakness in Australia and New Zealand – are largely ignored foretastes of much worse to come.

The bear market in property in some of these countries – only nascent, and as foreseen in our first book *Wake Up!* – could last for up to ten years. But evidence is now emerging that in countries where inflation is being deliberately stoked – the US and the UK in particular – the bear market, while of the magnitude we forecast, could recover faster than we hitherto thought.

We mentioned in the first edition of our book that this was a wide world and that there would always be a bull market somewhere. There are opportunities aplenty out there in real estate. You just have to know where to look.

These opportunities are now expanding because of the ferocious price falls in many markets. But let's reiterate firstly our buy recommendation on one property market – and that's Germany. This is the only market of substance that we see as not having declined in terms of residential accommodation prices in the 'Great Correction' – and we continue to see tremendous upside here with limited risk.

First though, let's share with you how we stumbled upon Germany as a real estate investment opportunity.

The search for investment opportunities can take odd forms …

In late 2004, Jim went on a trip to Israel to investigate local stock market opportunities. He met some very smart people in Tel Aviv, who told him that the markets locally were looking overheated. One or two of them mentioned, however, that they had been buying property in Germany.

Germany? How dull that seemed.

A G8 country, then going through a sort of grinding recession, partly as a result of the cost of reunification in the early 1990s as well as the wage-squeezing effect of entry into the euro at too high a rate for the Deutschmark.

Germany was also undertaking some major labour market reforms, designed to restore its competitiveness and to try and kick start really anaemic growth.

A variety of factors had pushed German residential property prices down in nominal terms – and quite a long way down in inflation-adjusted real terms. These factors included a poorly developed mortgage market, the fact that Germans were used to a rental rather than ownership culture, and the fact that East Germany in particular had a high proportion of 'worker' and municipal housing.

So by 2005 German property prices were amongst the worst performing in the world over a 15-year period, and certainly were the cheapest amongst all developed nations.

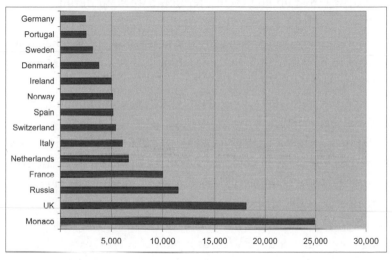

European Average Residential Price (€/Square metre). Reproduced by permission of www.globalpropertyguide.com

German property prices hovered at levels below their fundamental replacement cost – in certain cities, well below – and that excluded the value of the land.

To put that in perspective, Berlin property sold at less than 10 per cent of the cost, foot for foot, metre for metre, than London property – and it's still not far off that level.

Jim did some basic research and set off in his car in a ferry across the English Channel in search of opportunity in Germany.

First stop – Hamburg. But wait; whereas in the UK, the US or Australia every second shop is a real estate office with pictures displayed of properties for sale, in Hamburg he couldn't find a single such office. In fact, he had to go to the town hall and ask for the name of an agent – and got short shrift and a copy of the Yellow Pages for his trouble.

Anyway, to cut a long story short, Jim and his friend Anthony Baillieu who was on the trip with him (and a much better driver), eventually tracked down the offices of an agent and started looking around, first in Hamburg then, later in the week, in Berlin.

Wow, what bargains were to be found.

Properties were selling at 9 per cent plus rental yields, when it was possible to borrow at 4.5 per cent (though it has to be said getting mortgages wasn't that easy).

Properties were then selling at one third the cost of building them, with full occupancies. Properties built as rental units, typically of 30–50 apartments or so, in good areas, well maintained, and freehold. Properties where rents could be raised by up to 20 per cent every three years and where the typical rent was a much lower fraction of total income of the tenants than in, say, the UK or the US.

A *BigIdea* in the making.

So, how to go about it? Well, as it happened, Jim was invited to a friend's wedding where he met just the person – Florian Lanz – to help him build a business around German property.

Florian knew all the players, was highly experienced and, like Jim, thought property prices were too cheap. So he, along with one of Jim's colleagues from the UK, Justin Rose, helped Jim assemble a portfolio of buildings in and around Berlin that now amounts to about 3000 flats and which was bought at an average yield (i.e. rent divided by purchase price) of 9 per cent and where the borrowings that support it carry fixed interest rates for seven to ten years of 4.5 per cent.

So, in other words, Jim is being paid to hold these properties, even after paying the interest on the loans, which in part have enabled him to make these purchases.

Having started buying, Jim and an old university friend of his, Bob Macdonald, set about bringing this *BigIdea* – that German property represented the best major market real estate opportunity in the world – to a wider audience.

That wider audience took the form of subscribers to a series of funds that Jim and Bob's fund management company have launched to take advantage of the German anomaly.

These funds, launched by the Speymill Group out of the UK, now consist of $3 billion plus of assets, and 45,000 apartments all over Germany, managed by a team of 300 people based in Berlin.

All of this has happened since 2005.

And it has happened because of a combination of factors – all leading to a single *BigIdea*. In fact, a *BigIdea* that has become a *Money-Fountain*.

These factors include:

1 Listening to others – Germany wasn't Jim's idea. He got it from listening to smart people, in the unlikely surroundings of an Israeli stockbroker's office.
2 Going and doing further research yourself – and quickly. *BigIdeas* don't remain exclusive for long.
3 Having the luck of meeting the right people to make it happen. This is where social networking meets business success.
4 Moving quickly to establish a position in the *BigIdea*.

Now, the reason why we are harping on about this German property idea is that although prices have moved up a little – and, as a result, yields have come down a tad – this remains perhaps the finest *BigIdea* we have in real estate. It was at the time of the initial publication of this book – and it still is.

We believe that the German story will run and run.

Here are our reasons why:

1 Germans, for so long convinced that renting was better than buying, are beginning to change their minds. Mortgages, partly through new competition introduced by non-German banks, are becoming much more available in Germany, so the key factor in the Anglo-Saxon housing boom of the past two decades – the availability of credit – is now being introduced into Germany.

2 Property in Germany is still by far the cheapest in terms of per square foot or metre price of any developed nation.

3 Property 'yields' are still substantially above the cost of borrowing. Only Japan shares this characteristic. This is beginning to change in the UK and the US also – and hence buying opportunities are beginning to emerge there too.

4 Construction volumes have been moribund in Germany for some time but net household formations are growing. In the next 15 years the numbers of German households – due to immigration, divorce and longer life expectancy – is expected to rise to 42 million, an increase of 10 per cent over today. So few homes are being built that the existing housing stock will *have* to rise in price.

5 The German economic machine is, along with all other countries, slowing down due to a global recession – but Germany is by far the most productive and efficient country in the euro zone. Germany has squeezed costs – in contrast to France and Italy it has a current account surplus, it has once again grown faster than France, and it is the world's largest exporter.

All told, these are factors that we think will make German property – and residential property in particular – a really good place for people to have money over the next ten years.

And we are going to show you how to make that investment in a way that doesn't involve the hassle of finding physical property, of arranging mortgages, of dealing with the local tax regime, of managing tenants, or of even going to Germany.

We are recommending that investors look at a range of relatively large companies (in terms of assets at least, as all are selling at big discounts to their asset values) listed on the London and German Stock Exchanges which have assembled fine portfolios of German residential or commercial property and which provide the ideal exposure for investors seeking to invest in German real estate. We detail this approach below.

But before we do, let us emphasize that the point of the German real estate story is that ideas for investors – the ones that are not just the generally parroted ones of the popular press – tend to come out of left-field.

But once a good idea has been researched, and a way of implementing it has been found, it can take shape as something real and of important value to the creation of long-term wealth.

Germany remains a top pick of ours in terms of real estate. It is a large market, with established laws and practices, and it has finally broken out of a very long-term bear market.

In our experience, real estate cycles are much longer than those of stock. A bull market has established itself in the German property market, just as the sun has set on the US, UK, Spanish and Australian property markets. That bull market in Germany should be exaggerated in its upwards tendency by the inflationary measures being taken by major central banks – including the European Central Bank. This is the same fuel that will reverse the downwards move in certain Anglo-Saxon markets sometime in 2010, but in contrast to them, the German market will NOT HAVE FALLEN during the 'Great Correction'.

But let's get back to the practicalities of how to access the market itself.

Of course, you could fly to Berlin, or Frankfurt, Munich, Hamburg or any other German city, and buy a flat or a block of flats – but in practice this is not as easy as it sounds.

For a start, the real estate agents are expensive (about 6 per cent commission for an individual buyer – yes, in Germany the buyer pays the commission), there are notary (or legal) fees, and there's a real estate transaction tax of about 3.5 per cent. So all in all, as an individual investor you are looking at about a 10 per cent cost of getting into the market.

On top of that there are all sorts of tax issues relating to income and capital gains; the difficulty of getting a mortgage if you are a foreign individual investor; and lack of clear advice as to what is the best solution for you.

This is where what we just talked about earlier in this section comes into play – proxies for real estate.

Rather than buying property directly, for Germany, we recommend that you buy shares in a fund or company that specializes in real estate in that country.

Broadly speaking these shares fall into two categories: residential or commercial.

Although there are funds that invest in all types of real estate throughout Germany, it may be best to invest in the more specialized operators.

These funds generally have access to much better leverage, i.e. borrowing, than individual investors and on better terms. They tend to have a much more diversified portfolio than that available to individual investors. In other words, they own a multiplicity of buildings, generally speaking throughout Germany, although some specialize in just one area, most commonly in Berlin.

They generally have established rental and accounting procedures, and they tend – in the case of those operated on behalf of investors outside Germany – to have worked out ways of being tax-efficient *vis-à-vis* the German tax code.

Of course, nothing is for free and the fund managers charge fees – a bit like on stock funds – which typically will consist of an annual management fee plus a performance fee.

Most of these funds are 'closed ended' – in other words, they trade on recognized stock exchanges – and generally speaking, the London or German Stock Exchanges. This is because 'open ended' or daily or weekly traded funds – where investors can redeem their holdings at will based on the fund's net asset value – do not lend themselves easily to real estate investment. After all, buildings are not as easy to sell as shares or bonds, so if everyone wanted to get their money out at once it would be difficult to liquidate the portfolio of real estate to satisfy them.

These closed end funds generally have a 'life'. That is, they have fixed dates by which time they are likely to wind up, so investors taking a similar view to us would be best off investing in one that has a life that matches their own investment horizon.

Most of these funds have been affected by the decline in real estate across the world and by the broad sell-off in shares, so most of them now sell at large discounts to their asset values. However, in many cases we do not see any impairment coming to these asset values, since we believe that German residential prices have not gone down, making them an even better buy than at the time our book was first published.

BigIdea # 4

In our opinion, it would be best if investors take the longest possible view of German real estate. The bull market has just started and, based on our overriding principle of 'riding one's winners', this investment is one to hold on to for the long term.

Furthermore, most of the funds pay or will eventually pay dividends from surplus rental income left over after their costs of operation (interest and management expenses). As a result, investors are being 'paid' to hold the German real estate assets that comprise the funds' holdings.

These funds tend to trade on stock markets so the best thing for investors to do is to seek professional advice as to which one is best for them.

As with any investment, the key factors to look out for are:

• the reputation of the management of the fund;
• the extent to which it is already invested, whether or not the fund sells at a discount or premium to its NET ASSET VALUE (the

value of the fund's assets divided by the number of shares in issue – and they almost all sell at substantial discounts);

- the dividend YIELD of the fund (the dividend it expects to pay over the share price, i.e. a fund paying a 6 cent dividend with a US$1 share price has a dividend yield of 6 per cent); and
- how much the manager charges – are the management fees reasonable and is the manager incentivized through a performance fee for the bulk of her reward?

Then there is the issue of where the fund invests; residential property in Germany is in most ways more attractive than commercial, in our opinion, because it sells on average at below replacement cost and there is a developing shortage. Commercial property on the other hand is easier to manage, has more predictable income streams and is keyed in terms of price to the growth of the overall German economy. We provide a list of possible investments to review at the end of this section.

We recommend, as one of our *BigIdeas*, a mix of two-thirds residential and one-third commercial. We also suggest that German property can reasonably be as much as half of your non-home (i.e. your own house) property portfolio.

In terms of how much you should have in real estate as a percentage of your total investment, please refer to the *DiagnosticGrid* that comes with this book, which will provide a recommendation based on your own particular circumstances.

Other areas of real estate investment opportunity to consider are:

- Macau
- Brazil
- Japan

with Macau as the clear standout.

These three areas have great potential in our opinion, but Macau with Germany would provide a good long-term mix for investors.

Macau is fast developing as the Las Vegas of Asia – except on a bigger and potentially more profitable scale. It is a small enclave in Southern China, adjacent to Hong Kong, and is the only place in China where legalized casino gambling takes place. Huge investment is going into the territory to the extent that on many measures Macau overtook Las Vegas in 2007. The territory offers fantastic residential property investment opportunities, but not without risk, and this is a more speculative recommendation.

Again, the only effective way for a foreigner to play this opportunity is via funds or companies involved in local property and we mention a couple of those later.

Brazil is an interesting emerging market play. India, on the other hand, is suffering from an acute over-speculation in real estate. Of course, both of these countries are beginning to play catch-up to China, which in some ways has developed an unhealthily overheated market in real estate. Eighty per cent of Chinese households in urban areas own their own homes and, although only half of all such homeowners have a mortgage, there have been some signs of acute speculative activity. Chinese prices have begun to fall sharply in line with most of the rest of the developing world.

In other ways, for instance the ratio of real estate prices to income per head, Chinese real estate doesn't look nearly as bad. But we have yet to be convinced that this is the most effective way to 'play' China as a *BigIdea*, and for that reason we confine ourselves to exposure to China as a BRIC economy through a well-managed fund (see the BRIC *BigIdea* on p. 146 in Chapter Six).

Both Brazil and India are developing large middle classes, which are the principal drivers of the housing booms that are likely to continue in these countries for some decades to come. Both are speculative markets, with some political and execution risk, but nonetheless, we recommend that for a smallish portion of overall real estate exposure, some money be devoted to one of them – i.e. Brazil – again through funds.

This is because in India, prices have already risen at a level that far surpasses the growth of other emerging property markets, and for longer. From 2002–2006 the average price of real estate in India rose by 16 per cent per annum, well ahead of the growth in average income. Prices of equivalent apartments in Mumbai are about three times of those in Shanghai and not much less than in Tokyo.

Brazil, on the other hand, is fast becoming a really serious economy, and property prices are fractions of those of the more overheated markets of Asia – and there is a desperate and critical shortage of housing.

The two key markets we like, though, are Germany for the bulk of overseas property exposure, and Macau for a smaller, more dynamic holding.

Investors might also look at some investment in Japanese property which, apart from anything else, will have the advantage of giving them exposure to the Japanese yen, although a large part of our targeted appreciation in that currency has taken place.

Japanese property has been in the doldrums for a long time, although residential property has recently attracted some interest as Japan's economy has begun to emerge from a deflationary period and as yen borrowing costs have remained very low.

Commercial property in some areas has also begun to move upwards, but there remain pockets of opportunity. Japan is, in some ways, a bit like Germany – a behemoth economy that lost its way. The economy still stumbles along, and is being affected by the credit crunch, but fundamentals of Japanese real estate look promising. Once a bull market is established in Japan it could last for a very long period. The difference between Germany and Japan, however, is that Japanese property still sells at a premium to replacement cost, making it fundamentally less compelling than German property. This is because of the acute shortage of buildable land in Japan.

Real Estate Investment Trusts (REITS) – which started life in the United States in the 1960s – have now sprung up in many other countries. They are tax-attractive vehicles designed to encourage property investment in specific sectors of economies, typically by offering a tax advantage to individual and institutional investors.

Although the rules vary somewhat from one country to another, generally speaking REITS distribute the bulk of their net surplus income (rents minus management and interest expenses) without paying corporation tax on such income. This means that investors don't pay tax twice – once as tax on company profits, and once by way of an income tax on their dividends.

They have become popular in Japan, Hong Kong, Australia, and France. They have also recently been introduced to the UK and to Germany.

In some cases they can be attractive, and enhance returns for investors looking to make an investment. They should, however, never be bought solely because of their tax advantages.

Investors, when considering real estate investment, should first and foremost consider the important factors detailed above before committing.

Tax issues should be a secondary consideration.

To recap, those IMPORTANT considerations should be:

1 The macro cycle – perhaps the most important element in considering real estate.
2 The affordability ratios and replacement cost factors.
3 The ease, or otherwise – via funds most likely – of making an investment in an unfamiliar jurisdiction.

These predominate as the reasons to make or not to make real estate investments.

In terms of shares that give exposure to these investments, we recommend readers consider the following:

Germany – Commercial Properties
DIC Asset (symbol DAZ:GR)
An owner of large blocks of Frankfurt office buildings. Yield forecast at more than nine per cent on dividend in euros.

Germany – Residential

Speymill Deutsche Immobilien Company (symbol: SDIC:LN)
London-listed fund with €1.4 billion mostly invested in German residential property. Yield forecast at ten per cent, and management (affiliated with Jim) is very competent.

Germany – Diversified

Puma Brandenberg (symbol: PUMA:LN)
London-listed fund invested in residential, commercial and mixed-use real estate. Twenty-five per cent of the fund is invested in Berlin residential.

Macau

Speymill Macau Fund (symbol: MCAU:LN)
London listed. A well-positioned fund controlling some US$400 million of assets in Macau residential property, all bought at good prices. Has links to excellent local partners and good prospects. This fund is also affiliated with Jim who is the largest shareholder of the manager, Speymill Group plc.

Macau Property Opportunities Fund (symbol: MPO:LN)
A US$300 million, London-listed fund engaged in property development and investment in Macau and China's Pearl River Delta. The fund is managed by Sniper Capital Limited.

Brazil

As far as Brazil is concerned, there are a number of Brazilian home-builders listed on the Brazilian stock exchange, but we would recommend that investors wait until a reputable UK or US manager brings out a dedicated fund for Brazilian property. Take a look at that when it emerges as a way to play this very interesting market.

ChapterFour

Stocks and Mutual Funds

For just about anyone, stocks are a vitally important part of a long-term investment strategy. Mutual funds, or other collective schemes such as unit trusts or investment trusts, represent a convenient method for time-short non-investment professionals to invest in the stock market.

But, without a doubt, stock investment is the hardest of all investment classes to undertake successfully on a long-term basis.

This is partly because stocks are subject to a panoply of variables – economic cycles, stock market sentiment, individual corporate performances and valuation issues to name just some. Analyzing any of these is time-consuming and knowledge-intensive. And even if time and knowledge is available, there is no certainty that the right choices will be made. The events of 2008 bear this out – companies folding, stock markets crashing and all the old certainties ruptured in a volcanic financial eruption.

But investors reading this book shouldn't throw their hands in the air and just give up. Nor should they resort to the 'dartboard' method of choosing stocks, or wildly chase 'tips', or even put their faith entirely in the hands of a mutual fund or hedge fund manager. After all, clients of Mr 'made-off with the money' Madoff didn't exactly enjoy Christmas 2008, having been swindled out of $50 billion. So it seriously is worth making the effort to get the stock part of your portfolio right. It is worth selecting the mutual funds and/or shares that have a better chance of success over the long term, because their performance – probably more than that of any other asset class – will make a substantial difference to your portfolio.

This is because 'stocks' or 'shares' represent the ONLY form of investment that is the pure reflection of cumulative human endeavour.

What do we mean by this?

Well, a 'share' is simply that; it is a bit of paper (now more likely to be electronically registered, of course) representing a piece or partial ownership of an enterprise. This enterprise will consist of human beings and capital (money, equipment and property) engaging in a commercial activity – for profit.

That enterprise will grow or fail based on the efforts of its management and employees to maximize the use of that 'capital'.

The capital is what belongs to the shareholders and, ultimately, capital can consist of a whole variety of things: plant and equipment; buildings; computers; and of course, 'intangible' property such as brands, trademarks or patents.

The 'stock' issued by the corporation has been sold (or given) at some past date, in the form of shares in itself. This can have been either in order to raise capital or for the acquisition of the capital of another enterprise; alternatively, it could have been for the issue of shares to employees or managers as an incentive.

A stock market is just a forum (and normally now, an electronic one) in which shares are traded.

A company's shares are 'listed' if they are introduced onto a recognized (or regulated) stock exchange, e.g. the London Stock Exchange (LSE) or the New York Stock Exchange (NYSE).

Stockbrokers are agents who trade shares on behalf of others – and often for themselves – on stock exchanges. Typically, stockbrokers are 'members' of an exchange, which qualifies them to engage in such trading. Stockbrokers charge 'commissions' – which can vary wildly – to execute such trades. In addition, many stockbrokers, particularly the larger ones which describe themselves as 'investment banks', act as 'principals'.

This means that they trade stocks using their own money and quite often investors will find themselves buying stocks directly from their stockbroker's 'book'. This is a practice which prompts us to recommend to our readers that they always leave a so-called 'limit order' with their broker – in other words, never or only in exceptional circumstances, give the trade price to the 'discretion' of a broker. They may end up lining their pockets even more at your expense if you do. A limit order is simply one where you specify the maximum price at which you will buy a share, or the minimum price at which you will sell it.

The composition of listed enterprises differs widely between countries (based on each nation's corporate law) as well as within countries.

All sorts of stock can be issued – the most prevalent is **common** (or 'ordinary') stock, which is the simplest representation of collective ownership of a corporation.

This is where, as an example, a company has 100 shareholders, each one owning one share. The company therefore has 100 shares 'in issue', each one of them representing a claim to 1 per cent of the ownership of the company. These shares have an equal claim on the assets of the company after its debts and other obligations (e.g. tax) have been discharged and an equal right to whatever dividends are declared by the company.

But there are all sorts of other forms of share ownership, which readers may already be familiar with.

There are **preferred shares**, which entitle the holder of that particular class to a prior claim on the company's assets over and above the claims of a common shareholder.

There is **convertible bond debt**, where a bond (or fixed obligation – see Chapter Five) is issued by a company but where the bond may ultimately be convertible into common shares of the company. This is a kind of hybrid form of 'equity' or share.

Then there are **warrants** and **options**, which ascribe the right to the holders to buy shares in a company's common shares at a fixed price sometime in the future; there are deferred shares, typically issued to employees or management, and different types of shares depending on their voting rights.

But the most important one of all is the common share, which is also the most widely available to investors throughout the world, as well as the one that principally concerns us here.

The common share is so important to us because owning a share of a company is the only way that we can participate in the real growth of an enterprise. Gold, real estate, collectables, art, bonds, etc. are all valid and important investment strategies, but they don't grow – only their prices rise or fall. Once a building is built, to all intents and purposes it is finished. Its value may go up or down but it remains the same building.

Gold is just a lump of metal which has ascribed value to it in human terms. But the lump (despite the best efforts of alchemists everywhere) doesn't expand.

The only vehicles that can grow (except for governments, in which we can't and wouldn't choose to invest) are corporations.

This is because the corporation is always a work in progress, it is a living thing – competing, expanding, contracting – and reflecting the efforts of its stakeholders. By stakeholders, we mean shareholders, customers and employees.

Valuing shares and investing in them is difficult.

Identifying shares that will perform, i.e. go up over the long term, is even harder. But the effort is worthwhile because ultimately shares will be a key component of our long-term financial security, if we are to enjoy such a thing.

The simple definition of a share's value indicates that a stock is nothing but the net present value of a company's future earnings and dividends. In other words, if you know how much a company is going to make in terms of profits (or 'earn', in stock market parlance) and you can forecast its growth for some years out, and you can work out what inflation will be over that period and what value the stock market will ascribe to shares of its type, then investing in shares should be easy. Phew!

Simple, isn't it? Except that it's not.

Many people will tell you that investing in shares has been the best way to make money over a long period of time. And that is true if you happen to live in countries where records of continuous stock market investment exist for long periods of time.

This is because there is a so-called 'survivorship bias' in examining share results over the longer term. The long-term views of stock market performance takes into account only those markets that still exist. Sure, investment in the US or UK stock markets has bested just about every other form of investment over extended periods. It would be surprising if it had not done so as both economies have grown almost uninterruptedly for decade after decade, and higher Gross Domestic Product (GDP) generally speaking, and self-evidently, means more profit potential for the corporations operating within a country. This steady state of affairs has of course been disrupted by recent financial events – and the failure of behemoth companies such as Lehman Brothers, Bear Stearns and of course AIG – as well as the partial nationalization of large parts of the banking systems in almost every country of substance.

But long-term views of stock markets tend to ignore those markets which no longer exist: the pre-revolutionary Russian stock market, for instance, or the Argentinian stock market up until the Second World War (both markets have subsequently been revived but with all the original participants wiped out).

Or take for example pre-war German stocks – or any number of other markets where investors have been 'wiped out' by cataclysmic events.

In other words, because these 'bad' market results are excluded from studies showing just what a great thing stocks are, we end up with this 'positive' bias.

Also, a backwards examination of individual corporate and mutual fund performance tends to only look at the records of the survivors.

This positive bias means that we tend to focus our hindsight view of what has and what has not been a good investment on those shares that still exist in some form or other – or on those mutual funds that still exist. We discount those that have gone bust (in the case of corporations) or have retired, hurt, from the game (in terms of mutual or hedge funds).

At one stage in late 2008 it looked to some investors that such a cataclysmic event was going to happen on a global scale, and phrases such as 'nothing will ever be the same again' were being bandied around by the more lugubrious commentators. Some of these were the same ones who had failed to see the credit crunch coming, and they are in our view just plain wrong. We are in a cyclical downturn whose length will be curtailed by aggressive governmental intervention. That means that stocks, many of which sell at the time of publication at excessively low valuations, represent a compelling part of any investor's portfolio.

However the events of 2008 do demonstrate that although stocks are generally a good investment, the view of stocks generally has perhaps been too rose-tinted – and a strong caveat emptor view of them should be applied by all investors.

So, the common view that equities are unquestionably the only long-term 'safe bet' investment is erroneous. In some cases, they can be a very unsafe bet indeed. The 'wipe-out' markets are testimony to this – and of course the 'annus horribilis' of 2008 for equity investors almost everywhere.

It's easy to say with perfect hindsight that investors should have seen it coming – but the owners of those shares, which were destroyed in value, were in possession of all the facts. What they missed was knowledge of what former Defence Secretary Donald Rumsfeld once called the 'unknown unknowns'.

Rumsfeld, in using this phrase, was paraphrasing Nassim Taleb, whose two books *Fooled by Randomness* and *The Black Swan* brilliantly explain the fact that none of us has a perfect view of what will happen in the future. And it is to our peril if we begin to believe that we can see ahead.

It may seem obvious, but he relates it cleverly to the way in which many people place blind trust in the continuation of the past – for instance that Company X will continue to grow because it has done so in the past, or that Fund Manager Y will always outperform the indices because he or she has in the past.

Although the past is a useful guide to *certain* characteristics of the likely pattern of the future, it is by no means an infallible guide.

Taleb says that even the greatest investors will at some stage be 'FOOLED BY RANDOMNESS'. In other words, they will be undone by something they cannot hope to foresee – simply because it is not foreseeable.

So, an important lesson for investors in stocks is never, ever extrapolate that the future will be like the past. It won't be.

That doesn't mean that the management, either of companies or of mutual funds, shouldn't be judged by what they have done in the past. Backing outright novices might just work out, but it's taking a big gamble.

The tried and tested tend to continue to perform according to past patterns, but those patterns can and often are interrupted by events that we cannot foresee.

That is why diversification is a key factor, particularly in stock markets. Because the 'impossible' has an inconvenient habit of actually occurring, in theory the wider the portfolio of shares that you own, the more likely your chance of surviving any individual event which might affect any individual share price.

Of course if the 'impossible' is an event that is cataclysmic for an entire stock market, nothing will save your portfolio – at least in the short term.

But being diversified internationally, as well as through sectors and companies in your own stock market, makes a great deal of sense. The more eggs you have in your investment basket, the more of them that are likely to hatch. It's simple arithmetic.

Except there is such a thing as TOO much diversification. That's because if you have a bit of everything you will do no better or worse than the generality of markets. You might as well be in a so-called INDEX fund, one that tracks the indices of various markets. In fact, in certain circumstances, these have investment merit as quick and easy ways of gaining market exposure – and they are generally managed at low cost.

For exposure, for instance, to markets that are relatively alien to your own home market – an emerging market or a particular sub-sector of a market, index tracking funds can make good sense.

But to really build wealth – and build some of it using the stock market – you have to work harder – or make your fund managers work harder – than just putting your hard-earned cash into an index product.

Let us first say that we are NOT market gurus and don't pretend to be. In fact, we strongly advise people not to slavishly follow what such types say or do. Even someone like Warren Buffett, whose record is the most estimable of all, isn't going to show his full hand for you to follow. And those people who write tip sheets and suchlike do so, probably, because they are not Warren Buffett.

That having been said, we do believe in seeking as much information as is possible for you to absorb and to commit time to sifting through. Our natural HEURISTICS or filtering mechanisms will allow us to get to grips with information, we hope, without becoming totally overwhelmed.

Information for time-constrained people can come through a variety of sources. Magazines, books, newspapers and television, the Internet – you name it – there is an abundance of information out there.

But how should you decide – assuming that you are not an investment professional – just which bits to concentrate on? As we said, we are not market gurus, but we do have very specific words of advice for our readers.

1 Focus on two or three *BigIdeas* for your stock and mutual fund portfolio. We will explain how to generate these later on.
2 Having developed this focus, avoid all the 'noise' that comes with market commentary, market updates, short-term stock market movements, etc. Very little of that will make you money. Mostly, it will encourage you to trade – which is one of the big destroyers of value. Trading makes money for brokers – it doesn't tend to make money for private investors.
3 Evolve a style of your own when evaluating shares and mutual fund managers. Our own recommendation will be to reflect at least one or two of your *BigIdeas* through individual shares, which you follow closely, and for the rest to be represented by mutual fund or collective scheme investment. We shall explain below.
4 Remember that using RULES can be an effective way of adding discipline to your investment process, but that method, i.e. slavishly following a checklist of 'orders', won't always work. Look what happened to Long Term Capital Management in 1999, for instance; its famous 'black box' theory of investment, where a whole load of Nobel Laureates and other smart people developed a 'formula' for investment success, was undone by a series of random events, which even these clever chaps couldn't foresee. Look at all those suave 'fund of fund managers' who were fooled by Mr Bernie Madoff without doing in-depth due diligence before selecting his firm.

Another example of humility being forced on the self-styled smart guys was, of course, Enron – at one stage one of the largest companies in the United States.

In a way, the market is a bit like the sea: useful if treated with respect, but utterly cruel if crude attempts are made to 'tame' it.

So, with that caveat, what are our specific recommendations as to how people should construct that portion of their investment portfolio devoted to stocks and to stock-based mutual funds?

In terms of seeking the *BigIdeas*, the first thing to do is to remove yourself from your normal surroundings – work, the home, anywhere that is familiar to you – and spend a full day writing down what you think – from your reading and your experience of the real world – are the **next three big things**. These will be your very own *BigIdeas*.

You don't have to be original; you just have to think carefully about what you come up with. There are over 6.7 billion people in the world, and it's unlikely that any one of us is going to have an earth-shattering 'eureka' moment. It is more likely that human progress will come by gradual increments, improving on existing technologies bit by bit. And it is those types of ideas that are likely – if you follow our guidance – to be the lynchpin of your stock investment portfolio for the next ten years.

Well, what exactly constitutes a *BigIdea*?

It may be something directly related to your own area of expertise – and each one of us is likely to be an expert at *something*. Perhaps your own area of expertise might provide a clue as to one or more of the ideas you are thinking about.

We are all human beings – perhaps just thinking about our existence and place on the planet will give you some idea of what you should be looking at. Or perhaps your own reading will have provided you with some stimulus.

Don't just write down three things on as bit of paper and stagger off looking for opportunities. REALLY focus on your list, and concentrate on refining it. Take your time. It's very important.

What sort of things are going to shape our world in the next ten years? Who do I trust to give me guidance on this? What sort of commercial applications will spring up around us in relation to economic change? Which countries and sectors will be the best performing?

This is a form of self-examination; rather than just saying, 'Oh, I'll give all my money to Fred at Money-Makers Fund Management to look after,' what you are doing is developing your own world-view, one which you can then use to tailor your investment strategy.

With this list completed – and remember, it's best constructed in a place without personal distraction – go back home or to your office. And then start the process of working out just where those hard-earned dollars or pounds will go to reflect it.

But first – let's give you a few examples of what *BigIdeas* have occurred to us in the past and how *we* have reacted to them.

We wrote a book together about three years ago (entitled *Wake Up!*) and one of the themes of the book – which recurs in this one – is that the effects of climate change are here to stay, and that investment decisions worldwide will be in part shaped by our reactions to the potential climate crisis.

One of the things that we talked about was how – at least in the interim – nuclear power remained the cleanest, quickest and most practicable option for the world to pursue. But nuclear power depends on a fuel that two years ago was little talked about, hadn't been aggressively explored for a long period of time, and whose price was languishing at very low levels.

That fuel was uranium.

A little later, Jim was sitting in the pub that he owns in London (the 'Commander', in Notting Hill, if readers ever want an excellent watering hole), with a good friend of his, Steve Dattels.

Steve knows everything there is to know about the mining industry. He was a co-founder of American Barrick, one of the world's leading gold producers, and has created a multiplicity of successful companies.

The talk got round to *Wake Up!* and its mention of nuclear power. Steve said that he was thinking of putting together a uranium company and would Jim be interested in being his partner.

Jim – flattered to be asked by one of the mining greats – jumped at the chance. His and Steve's investment amounted that evening to less than US$150,000.

The *BigIdea* was to explore for uranium.

Not only was uranium going to be needed in greater quantity, as more nuclear power plants were being built (particularly in China), but Russian supplies of uranium, largely from the decommissioning of old nuclear weapons, were drying up. The price of uranium was low and the opportunity high. The perfect confluence for a *BigIdea*.

Steve knew the people to make it happen and he catalyzed a company which, after several rounds of finance and a listing on the London and Toronto Stock Exchanges, was sold after only two years for US$2.5 billion – yes, that's the correct figure.

Jim's early investment – thanks to Steve and his brilliant management team – is up almost an infinite amount.

That's because Steve mobilized top-flight executives, armed with capital that he raised from institutional investors, to buy licences to explore for uranium in Africa and elsewhere. By 2011 Uramin, as the company is known, will be one of the world's largest producers of uranium.

Over the period since Steve and Jim had that drink in the Commander pub, the price of uranium has risen by four times, making the foundation of the company all the more prescient.

A happy confluence of factors – a good idea, a terrific management team, a rising price for the product in question and healthy capital markets – enabled over US$400 million to be raised to fund exploration and ultimately mine production. All of these contributed to the amazing success of Uramin.

Although he's far too modest to claim sufficient credit for this amazing success, ultimately it's all down to one man – Steve Dattels.

But surely, you might well say – that was just a lucky break … getting things right on that scale doesn't happen often. The point is – it doesn't NEED to happen too often for you, dear reader, to end up with a lot more money than you started out with. Get just one of those *BigIdeas* right, and you have your very own *MoneyFountain*.

That's why just THINKING of your own list of *BigIdeas*, and waiting for or, even better, searching for the investment opportunity to match them to come along makes such good sense.

But what other *BigIdeas* might there be lurking out there? Well, as we said earlier, think about your own experience as a human being.

What do you notice around you? More people – yes, the world is expanding in terms of population, but unevenly so. This is leading to pronounced increases in migratory patterns from 'youth-rich' countries to those with deteriorating 'dependency ratios' (the number of workers in a society who support a typical dependent – children, old persons, disabled persons, etc.).

It is also noticeable to most of us in the developed world that our societies are aging – people are living longer and retirements, which once might have lasted a few years, can now occupy significant chunks of our lifespan.

These DEMOGRAPHIC factors are well known – but how do we take advantage of them? Well, consider the needs of older people as a starting point. Think about our earlier *BigIdeas* on this subject and develop your own train of thought.

Can/should elderly care be improved? The answer is yes, and whole new industries will spring up dedicated to the needs of the elderly. What about life quality and expectancy? Don't most people want to live longer?

In an era where the human genome has been sequenced, doesn't it make sense to think about the role of biosciences and preventative medicine in the modern world? Yes.

Are there any opportunities in this sector? Of course.

Other areas involving Big Pictures which might lead to *BigIdeas* include the earlier one of climate change. So let's think of the ways in which we might profit from that.

The first is obviously in industries designed to slow down that rate of change – and a whole chapter of this book will be devoted to just that area (Chapter Eight). Renewable energy, cleaner fossil fuel energy, fuel cells, and different transportation mechanisms – all of those provide an abundance of opportunity for us as investors and as human beings.

Then look at the issue of climate change from a different perspective – apart from industries devoted to its reversal, are there going to be any permanent effects on the way in which our societies are ordered as a result of warming temperatures? Of course. Let's look at the climates of countries which are going to be worst affected:

- Australia, for instance, is increasingly suffering from terrible droughts. It is entirely possible that more and more of the country will become a desert, leading to changed patterns as to where people will live. It is even possible that the bulk of the population of Australia may have to leave the country in the next thirty or forty years because of rising heat and lack of arable land. What effects will that have on Australia's domestic industries, on its real estate? The prognosis has got to be negative, of course.

- What about formerly very cold countries like Norway or even temperate countries such as the United Kingdom? One forecast we can make is that their climates will become progressively more attractive, relative to increasingly hot Southern Mediterranean countries, and that development will have two effects: it will make real estate more desirable in the currently cooler climes, and less desirable in the Southern Mediterranean.

- It will also probably make countries such as Spain and Greece, both dependent to a fair degree on tourism, less attractive to travellers and more vulnerable to economic downturns.

- Turning to the United States, the increased hurricane and flood activity we have seen in the past twenty years will become worse, and this will have significant ultimate effects on real estate prices – parts of the Americas will become less habitable, and real estate prices will fall. Furthermore, the benign conditions that the insurance industry has enjoyed in the last few years – reflect-ing rising premium rates as the effects of Hurricane Katrina have forced people to pay up for insurance – may be offset by an increasing rate of catastrophes on which insurance companies will have to pay out.

All of these events are interconnected to one *BigIdea* – that climate change will be a dominant feature of the investment landscape for a considerable time to come. This is whether or not you believe in it – and as we write this revised book in the chilly Northern Hemi-sphere winter of 2009, believers are thin on the ground. The fact is that climate change has become the 'zeitgeist' of our times, and because countering it represents massive infrastructural expenditure, governments around the world will increasingly spend money in this area. President Barack Obama has made energy independence a cen-tral plank of his platform of spending plans to counteract the credit crunch in the United States.

Bingo! We should look at ways of making money out of this area, especially as valuations have been compressed by the stock market malaise of 2008–2009.

Another *BigIdea* that we might look at is how the world's eco-nomic landscape is shifting. Almost anyone who can read knows that China is emerging as a global economic powerhouse, ultimately to rival the United States.

China's growth since the so-called 'Four Modernizations' began in 1979 has been breath-taking and China's influence on almost every sector of our world is increasing and will continue to do so.

Already, whole areas of the world's economic landscape have been altered as a result of China. Extractive or basic industries such as mining or steel production, once dismissed as cyclical and uninter-esting to investors, have been revived and transformed as a direct result of China's seemingly insatiable appetite for raw materials.

This appetite shows no long-term signs of diminishing, and the boom in commodities, largely sparked by China, has a long way to run, in our opinion. Of course, in the credit crunch, commodities have been badly hit, like everything else, and the short-term outlook is gloomy.

But isn't it better to be buying when all are fearful and the prices are low than when blue skies abound and investors have climbed on all the bandwagons and are about to wave goodbye to fortunes?

And of course, sneaking up on the sidelines are other Chinas or mini-Chinas – India, for example, whose population is likely to exceed that of China by the middle of this century; and Brazil, which is at long last beginning to show signs of promise.

In addition, even Africa, neglected by investors as a no-hope economic wasteland for so long, has been catalyzed by growth in its extractive industries (spurred by Chinese demands) and by the rapid dissemination of the mobile phone, which has facilitated communications. Africa is now in a new era of growth, and the continent as a whole seems capable now of 5 per cent plus GDP growth per annum for some time to come – even in the temporarily depressed economic conditions that we find ourselves in as we write.

Meanwhile the Anglo-Saxon and European economies continue to plod along, somewhat sclerotically, weighed down by inefficiencies, size and by high levels of debts and wages, while the balance of power shifts elsewhere. This is a long-term, immutable change that is not deflected by short-term economic cycles. It is a fact of life and, as the Americans would say – deal with it.

In that process of balance shift there are both dangers and opportunities. We detailed many of those dangers in our book, *Wake Up!*, but it's important not to overlook the many opportunities.

It's not necessarily the case that high GDP growth leads to high stock market returns, but it certainly helps companies and their profits if economic conditions are benign.

It's not yet the case that corporate governance and standards of transparency and accounting are as high in many developing countries as they are in the West or even in Japan, but growth rates are higher and opportunities abound.

For investment in the so-called BRIC economies – Brazil, Russia, India and China – it makes a lot more sense, in our opinion, to be diversified through an ETF or mutual fund of some sort than by trying to invest directly.

This is because – and despite the Internet – remoteness to the markets and unfamiliarity with the way in which they operate make it difficult for non-professional investors to devote the necessary time to make informed judgments on individual stocks.

In a short while, we will be addressing what to look for in a manager of funds investing in developing economies and indeed mutual fund managers investing elsewhere.

However, based on our experience, we would opt for more diversified funds – those that are 'pan-emerging markets' – rather than ones which are country- or region-specific. This is because, while we think it is important that every investor has some exposure to emerging markets over the longer term, it is very hard to judge which of those markets is most attractive at any given time.

Emerging markets are bottom drawer stuff (they're too racy to monitor on a monthly basis and you'll want to leave them for long periods at a time), so the selection of the manager is particularly important. You should regard an investment in emerging markets as one that you hold for AT LEAST ten years. In fact, if you were an emerging market investor in 2008 and were checking prices regularly, you're probably on beta-blockers by now!

And so that moves us on to the practical steps of implementing our *BigIdeas*.

Obviously not everyone is in a position to go off and start a new business based on their own 'world views' or *BigIdeas*. But there is a way in which you can come to some conclusions as to what you should do in practice:

1 Divide your *BigIdeas* into those that you can exploit by buying shares of companies which represent those ideas **directly on the stock market**, and into those which are best implemented by investing through a **mutual fund structure**.

   For simplicity's sake, we would recommend to our readers about a **fifty/fifty spilt** in this regard. In terms of how much of your investment portfolio should be devoted to shares or mutual funds investing in shares – please refer to the *DiagnosticGrid* which we discuss in Chapter Nine to cross-reference your own particular circumstances.

2 Let us assume that you really like the idea of investing in emerging markets. And further, that you have decided to follow our advice and stick to investing through a mutual fund for those particular investments. In those circumstances and in all other circumstances where you might invest in mutual funds, you need to do your homework.

   First of all, look to buy a fund that matches your own objectives – in other words, if you are looking for a spread of emerging market exposures, then select a fund that diversifies throughout the emerging markets.

   We also think that it is a good idea to be invested in a fund that is local to you: in other words, where the jurisdiction of its incorporation or that of the manager is where you are. If you are a UK investor, then go for a UK or British Isles-based fund. If you are American, go for a US fund – and so forth, if possible.

   This doesn't mean that the manager of the portfolio needs to be based physically round the corner from you. In fact, it may be better if they are based closer to the markets in which they are investing. But what it will do is to give you a legal and tax framework that is more appropriate to your individual circumstances.

   Investing internationally through a 'local' vehicle would be our strong advice. 'Local' to you, that is.

3 Choose a management company that is reputable, that has modest fees (but not too modest – otherwise they can't pay for the talent required to manage the portfolios), and one which is preferably free from a 'front end fee' (initial charge). There is absolutely NO reason why anyone should pay a commission to go into any mutual fund or unit trust. An initial charge can seriously eat into your returns over the long term and should be regarded as unacceptable. One of the things thrown up by the credit crunch is that you need to look for fund managers without debt on their balance sheet – in the US for instance, Lehman Brothers were big fund managers and went bust because of debt. In the UK, New Star, headed by the mercurial John Duffield, has effectively gone bust, and in Australia, Babcock and Brown is teetering on the cliff edge.

4 Check out the actual, that is, real life, manager of the fund you are thinking of investing in. Have they been with the firm for a while? Have they always been in the fund management business? Have they specialized in the area that they have invested in for a long time?

   Have they produced better than average REAL returns (i.e. after inflation) with low(ish) volatility? In other words, are they a safe pair of hands for your money? Remember, the first rule of money management is HOLD ONTO IT.

   Preferably, your manager should not be known for a flamboyant lifestyle, but should be on the road visiting companies often and should regard the management of money almost as a vocation – not as a lifestyle facilitator.

5 It is also important that your manager does not manage too much money. One of the few advantages open to a private investor in competition with the large institutional, pension and hedge funds who dominate most stock markets is that they can be more nimble and can invest in smaller companies than the big boys.

This one is self-evident – too much money means that fund managers have to diversify their portfolios into too many stocks. They thereby can lose focus, and they may also have to concentrate on the shares of larger companies, which because of their relative size have less room to grow.

Sure, there are a few companies which can continue to grow year after year, but they are few and far between. The facts of the matter are that, as companies get to be very big, they begin to suffer from the following ailments:

- Their lines of communication become extended. In other words, they have branches, offices and plants everywhere and it becomes harder and harder to control the proliferation of operations.
- They tend to develop internal bureaucracies that can – and often do – become increasingly ossified, acting as drags on growth.
- They find limitations to their natural growth simply because they are big relative to their markets – and as a result their performance becomes much more closely attuned to GNP growth or the growth of prices in their own market place.

Of course, investing in larger companies isn't necessarily a bad thing. If your *BigIdea* is 'steel', for instance, you may be best off investing in a large steel company, such as ArcelorMittal, which benefits from industry consolidation, fine management and economies of scale. But, conversely, Arcelor has a lot of debt which means that in a downturn, its fixed cost structure is highly vulnerable to falling steel prices and volumes.

Generally speaking, in selecting a mutual fund manager, you want him or her to have maximum flexibility in managing your money – if they manage so much money that they are CONFINED to larger companies as a matter of course in their investment decisions, then they have a serious strike against them to begin with.

So, in summary, ideally you are looking for a mutual fund manager who is local to you, but has wide investment horizons. One who has experience, but isn't swamped by money. One who regards each day at the office as a joy – not as a way to make a quick buck. Sounds good, doesn't it?

But how do you go about finding such a manager? Well, there are quite a few tools available to us.

Look at fund 'supermarkets' that now exist online in most developed markets; these generally offer no-load (i.e. no front-end fee) funds, or funds with greatly reduced entrance charges. For UK-based investors, the UK's largest fund supermarket is www.fundsdirect.co.uk. For Asia-based investors, you can consider www.fundssupermart.com. For US-based investors, there is www.morningstar.com.

Search Internet chat groups, newspaper and magazine reviews and rating agency reports (such as Morningstar) for appropriate management groups. Seek out as much information as possible; in other words, if you want to invest in a BRIC fund, look for guidance from as many sources as possible to understand who the real experts in that area are, who has the best record (not only recently, but over a timescale of five to ten years) and whether or not the individual manager has stayed with the particular firm for a good period (at least three years). Here are some of the online brokers you can visit to start your research (which can also be found in Appendix B):

United States	
Scottrade	www.scottrade.com
TD Ameritrade	www.tdameritrade.com
Schwab	www.schwab.com
E*Trade	www.etrade.com
Fidelity	www.fidelity.com

United Kingdom	
The Motley Fool Share Dealing Service	www.fool.co.uk (select 'Share Dealing' link towards the bottom of the page)
Halifax	www.halifax.co.uk (select the 'Share Dealing' tab from the menu bar)
Selftrade	www.selftrade.co.uk (click on 'Open an Account' at the top menu bar)
Interactive Investor	www.iii.co.uk (click on 'Register' at the top menu bar)
TD Waterhouse	www.tdwaterhouse.co.uk (click on 'Get Started' at the top menu bar)

Having identified one or two management firms, write to them and ask them to explain their investment philosophy and to give you a potted history of the firm. Most decent firms will be happy to oblige. Look at the prospectuses that they send you. Are the fees reasonable?

We judge about a 1 per cent annual management fee for an equity fund in developed markets to be reasonable; in emerging markets about 1.5 per cent per annum; for bond funds 0.5 per cent or less and for cash funds and for index funds (where the managerial duties are much less onerous) 0.25 per cent or less.

Look for hidden fees: extra advisory fees, transaction fees, etc. If they are there, ask the managers to explain them. They generally shouldn't be a feature of any halfway-decent manager.

While on the subject of fees, it's time for a quick commentary on hedge funds. Many investors regard these funds with an unnatural reverence. The reality is that hedge funds come in all sorts of guises and follow all sorts of strategies. What they typically have in common, though, is a tendency towards secrecy and, above all, a uniquely high set of fees.

The common parlance in hedge fund lingo is for '2 and 20'. This represents a management fee of 2 per cent per annum on assets managed and a 'performance fee', i.e. a share of profits, of 20 per cent per annum.

Let's look at the economics of this for a second by using an example.

If the Jeff Lardough Momentum Strategy Fund (it doesn't exist, so don't look for it), has US$1 billion under management and pursues a two and twenty strategy on fees, Jeff's personal economics look a little like this:

On an annual basis, Jeff will receive about $20 million dollars for the trouble of managing his client's money. He will have some expenses, of course: a couple of analysts, an office, a receptionist, a PA, computer terminals and some information services, but these probably won't cost that much relative to his fee income.

So we can safely say that if Jeff is the sole owner of his firm, he will walk away with $15 million every year for just showing up (assuming the clients stay the course).

But the real sex appeal of Jeff's business is his take on what many in the financial services business call OPM (Other People's Money). Jeff basically has a call option on the performance of his client's money.

It works like this: if Jeff's fund goes up, let's say by 30 per cent in a given year, before the clients can celebrate, Jeff deducts 2 per cent for his regular management fee. That leaves 28 per cent.

Then Jeff takes 20 per cent of that 28 per cent for himself, as a 'performance' fee – that's 5.6 per cent of the total fund at its start point for the year – or $56 million.

The bigger Jeff's fund is, the bigger his performance fee and the more sticks to his personal bank account.

So, the client's funds rose by 30 per cent during the year. But all that the client sees after deductions is 22.4 per cent. Not such an impressive outturn.

Jeff does pretty well, though – and it's no surprise that three hedge fund managers in the US were estimated to have made more than a billion dollars in take-home pay in 2006. The economics of the industry are very favourable to the managers.

Furthermore, just to scoop a bit more icing off the cake, a whole new – and large – industry has sprung up in recent years, known as the 'fund of funds' industry. This is where an investment advisory company constructs a portfolio on behalf of its clients, which consists of a series of investments in hedge funds and other 'alternative' strategies (private equity, venture capital, etc.).

There are typically two rationales for this service; first, that the fund of fund companies get 'access' to the best managers' funds which would be denied to other lesser-scale investors, and second, that by careful choice and diversification, the investor benefits from having made his or her own choices.

But this strategy carries a price – typically 1 and 10.

Yes, by now you've guessed that this is a 1 per cent annual management fee and a 10 per cent performance fee. And that's ON TOP of the 2 and 20 which is already making Jeff and his ilk so rich.

So if you add those up, you have a 3 and 30 take from the poor investor. This is a very high hurdle when you consider that all sorts of studies are suggesting that the proliferation of hedge funds in recent years has led to a diminution of their returns to clients. This has quite often been to the point that before fees they perform less well than the broad stock market indices.

Many hedge funds of course have 'blown up' in the market downturn of 2008. Sometimes being smart isn't enough and many were blindsided by such simple matters as counterparty risk (i.e. could the brokers or parties on the other sides of the trades they were doing actually pay – Lehman Brothers springs to mind here). In addition, many hedge funds were pursuing the same strategies, which became crowded, and when everyone headed for the exits at the same time, only a few managed to get out in time.

The fund of funds industry has been badly dented by its general failure to see that Bernie Madoff and his Ponzi (pyramid) scheme were about as suitable to investors as buckets of water to kittens.

The whole of the pricing, i.e. fee, structure of the hedge fund industry has been called into question by this debacle. Indeed, about half of all hedge fund assets have been lost either through redemptions or asset losses, and there are still a large number of investors trapped in hedge funds ('gated' as the industry coyly puts it).

In the first edition of this book we were sceptical about the sustainability of the hedge fund model – and it appears that we were right to be, although of course not all hedge funds should be tarred by the same negative brush.

One of the interesting things that we discovered in our research, however, was the disruptive nature of the new technique of getting around hedge funds' high fees – the so called 'replicator model'.

This innovative move has the potential to rock the hedge fund industry to its foundations – or at least to destabilize its cosy fee structure. This is on top of the lamentable performance of many hedge funds in 2008.

The academic Harry Kat, a Dutch economist, is the leading exponent of this new development and it has the potential to be very exciting.

Professor Kat realized that it would be impossible to accurately track exactly what leading hedge funds do – most hedge funds work in secret, and employ different and sometimes quite arcane techniques in their investment strategies. These strategies can rely on traders' instincts or on 'black box' computer-driven models to generate results.

Kat and his assistants backtracked data on 1900 hedge funds to come up with their investment ideas; that is, using a variety of sources they collated the past performance of a wide cross-section of the hedge fund industry and came up with the following conclusion: that the vast majority – that is at least 80 per cent – of hedge funds studied didn't outperform their relevant benchmarks. These benchmarks are the indices against which the funds and their investors measured their performance.

Kat's conclusion was that the cost of 'alpha' – the technical term for the outperformance by those funds – was negatively outweighed by the cost of fees. And given the generally egregious nature of hedge fund fees, that isn't very surprising.

So Kat and his business partner embarked on creating a pro-gramme known as Fund Creator, which simulates a wide variety of hedge funds and their styles with apparently amazing accuracy.

Fund Creator – for a tiny fraction of the fees charged by 'tradi-tional' hedge funds and with no so-called performance fees – can, with some little effort on the part of the user, do what many hedge funds do but at much lower cost. So the investor gets the same input as the majority of hedge funds, but with much higher returns.

This Fund Creator is really designed for big institutions looking for hedge fund diversification, not for individual investors. And, in fact, the very best hedge funds are hard to clone because the statistical data necessary to do so is just not there.

But the point of this commentary is that investors shouldn't get carried away by their mystical reverence for hedge funds. There are good ones – but there are a LOT of bad ones – and in our opinion, for most people, hedge funds are expensive and not useful.

If investors really want to get into hedge funds, some broker-ages now offer hedge fund 'tracker' funds, which seek to emulate the performance of different classes of hedge funds, rather than specific funds. These are, of course, provided at much lower cost than the types of funds that they seek to track. Goldman Sachs (www.gs.com) and Merrill Lynch (www.merrilllynch.com) are among the leading bro-kerages providing this service.

Remember, you are making a decision that will last you – we hope – at least ten years. You are investing with this firm for the future so take your time to make the correct choice.

Don't judge the performance of the fund over anything less than a two-year view. If the fund has disastrously underperformed its objec-tives over a period of over 24 months, then sell it.

Its objectives should be clear to you; to give you exposure to those *BigIdeas* where you think that mutual funds will serve you better than direct investment.

If, for instance, you have invested in a BRIC fund and the fund's Net Asset Value (the price at which you can buy and sell the shares) has remained flat but the relevant index has gone up 10 per cent, then – and only then – change managers.

Similarly, watch out for any change in the individuals managing your fund.

Watch the chat rooms – if you hear that Mr X, who managed your fund up until now, is leaving, then it is almost certainly a good idea to change funds. This is because – with the exception of index or tracker funds – investment management is part art and part hard work, and if a manager has generated good returns and he or she leaves, it is hard to replace them.

One increasingly popular form of investment – particularly in the United States – is called 'Exchange Traded Funds' (ETFs), which are shares that represent underlying baskets of assets, typically shares of a specific industry or country.

Transaction and management costs in these ETFs are low and they can be very worthwhile additions to a portfolio, substituting very well for some mutual funds. For instance, if your *BigIdea* is gold, there are ETFs that represent gold shares very well. ETFs are traded in the same way that shares are traded. We discuss a number of ETFs under our *BigIdeas* throughout the book.

So, having covered mutual funds, it's time to move onto **shares**. This is where the work gets a bit harder.

How do we choose the shares that best represent the *BigIdeas* that we have to chosen to invest in directly?

This is a hard – but very important – decision. It would certainly be a shame if you came up with the right *BigIdea* but chose the wrong shares to represent it.

We say 'SHARES' in the plural because putting all your money into one company's shares is a gamble too far, in our opinion. No matter how wonderful the share looks, something can go wrong. Remember the Black Swans.

In representing your *BigIdeas*, make sure that you DIVERSIFY. We recommend at least three stocks per *BigIdea*.

So, if you have three *BigIdeas* in total, we would recommend:

1 **Half** of your total stock market investment 'pot' invested in one diversified mutual fund, which represents **one** of the *BigIdeas*.
2 A **quarter** of the pot **divided into three shares** representing the second *BigIdea*.
3 A further **quarter** of the pot divided into three shares representing the third *BigIdea*.

That means that you will have half of your money set aside for share market investment in one mutual fund in the idea that is best represented by a mutual fund investment.

You will have chosen this fund very carefully, and will monitor its performance and its management very closely. This fund will, in itself, give you adequate diversification into a *BigIdea* that is too hard, too remote or too specialized for you to invest in directly through self-selected shares. This is because the fund's 'portfolio' will consist of a fair number of shares spread across the sector that you have chosen.

Then a further half of your 'stocks and mutual fund' money, apportioned into two other *BigIdeas*, will be divided into a total of six shares, which you will have selected with equal care and which you will monitor closely – but not too closely.

Remember, stockbrokers and other advisers want you to 'churn'. They like it when you 'trade' – because they can charge commissions and other fees.

Don't be tempted to trade by the fact that markets are fast-moving, however. If you've chosen a good portfolio, stick with it and don't be tempted to change it continuously.

On this subject let's look at some basic guides to stock market investment:

1 To repeat, don't be tempted to trade. In this respect, never ever listen to 'tips'. For most individuals these are a waste of time and should be avoided. Sure, some tips work, but sometimes the people who act on them end up in jail. This is because they may result from non-public information and that is illegal. Other 'tips' tend to be worthless, and indeed most generally lose money.

2 Don't buy options. Generally, the only people to make money out of these are the people who sell and trade them professionally. Options represent a right to buy a share (or to sell it) at a predetermined price for a relatively short period of time. There is whole panoply out there of options for investors to speculate with. Don't.

   We've been in the markets for a long time and can tell you that options just don't work. They normally pander to the short-term trader's gambling instinct; they are also expensive (the 'premium' you pay to get into them) and highly dependent on short-term factors that you just can't control.

3 Buy common shares in the companies you like and hold them. If your shares perform as expected – and give them at least a YEAR to do so – then RIDE YOUR WINNERS. All of us humans suffer from what is known as 'loss aversion'; that is, we don't like to lose. So, the average investors will SELL WINNERS to 'bag' profits, and buy more or continue holding 'losing' shares.

   This is understandable to all of us as human beings – none of us likes to admit that we were wrong – but it's entirely the worst strategy. You need to hold onto your winners (unless something fundamental has changed – and we will get to this is a moment). And most importantly you need to CUT your losers.

   By this we mean that if a stock persistently underperforms, and IF there are reasons why it is doing so (management changes, failure to meet earnings expectations, weakening markets or disappointing predictions, as examples) – then you shouldn't hesitate.

Sell the shares.

Winners sit on winning horses; and they ride them to the end of the course. That's what you, as a successful stock market investor, should do too.

What is likely to make a stock market winner? Well, anyone who ventures into the world of stocks will be bombarded from their first days and forever more with a whole long list of things they 'must' or 'must not' do.

Of course, we are adding to that list, but we hope in a positive and easy-to-understand way.

In this blizzard of information, you might come across 'Value Investing'; 'Growth Investment'; 'Modern Portfolio Theory'; and descriptions of managers as 'adding alpha' or 'beta' in market volatility, and even 'gamma'.

Phew.

You'll come across the 'unique secrets' of great investors – those of people such Warren Buffett, Sir John Templeton and George Soros, etc.

You will come across the various measures by which a company's performance is measured and their likely effects on the company's shares.

Some of these measures are as follows: PE Ratios (short for price to earnings ratios); PEG ratios (price to growth ratios); PBV (price to book value); and Quick Ratios (the ratio of net current assets on a company balance sheet to its net current liabilities – a measure of a company's solvency).

You'll be looking at inventories, gross margins, profit margins, profit per employee and a whole host of other accounting stuff.

Among these ratios, of course, is the often neglected debt to equity ratio – i.e. how much debt the company has relative to the funds owned by you, the shareholders.

Debt plus equity is known as the Enterprise Value of the business and is a measure that will be useful to you in your examination of what you should and should not buy.

You will even be met at the threshold of your stock market career by 'technical analysts'. These are people who generally use charts based on momentum, lunar cycles, long-term equation-based cycles, etc., which will tell you when you should buy and when you should sell.

All of these may be useful, of course, but we assume, dear reader, that you don't have the time or inclination to be a full-time stock analyst.

So what do you do?

Well, you have your two *BigIdeas* and you want to buy, let's say, six stocks that your research indicates best represents them. Let's get back to basics on this. How will those shares – assuming that you choose them carefully and correctly – ultimately reward you?

They will do so through a combination of CAPITAL GAIN and DIVIDENDS.

Capital Gain is the gain or profit you make over your purchase price – realization or sale proceeds minus cost.

Dividends are what you receive on an ongoing basis, hopefully. Dividends are typically expressed as a yield. In other words, if a company pays a dividend of 4 cents per share over a year, and its share price is 100 cents, then its yield is said to be 4 per cent.

Most growth companies don't pay any or much of a dividend because they typically can use the surplus cash – if any – generated by their business to grow it further.

These companies use money thus internally generated to buy new equipment, hire new people or to rent new premises, etc., so that the company can grow faster.

GROWTH – and for our purposes as capitalists and self-interested investors, we are looking here at growth in **profits** – is what we are seeking in our investments.

Because we are looking at *BigIdeas* and we hope that we are looking at them before the bulk of investors get to them (when they will
be welcome to buy us out at much higher prices), we are, in one sense,
GROWTH investors.

But we are also **VALUE** investors. Jim and Al don't like to pay
too much relative to the intrinsic value of a business and nor should
you. Like everything else, you should be choosy about finding good
value.

And we **are** picky – we also want the following things:

1 We want good, committed, experienced management – remember that shares reflect cumulative human enterprise and
management and employees will make the difference between
our investment being a good one or not.

2 We want businesses that are involved in saleable areas where
growth will not be limited by a small fundamental size – in
other words, it's all very well to invest in the best company
making some obscure item which has a limited market, but
unless they find new markets or develop new products, their
growth is going to be limited.

3 In that vein, we like companies which are not rooted to old
'centric' technologies – for instance, old-style telephony companies whose business, based on fixed wire technology, is quite
quickly being cannibalized by voice-over-Internet and by mobile telephony. We like companies whose products operate at
the EDGE of the network – that is where, as many will tell you,
the INTELLIGENCE now lies – and they're right. Old-style
ossified companies based on centralized production, or centralized systems, generally don't hack it any more.

4 Of course, that 'rule' may sometimes need to be amended or
ignored. Bear with us on this – it's not as confusing as it first
appears. People who dismissed cyclical industries like steel or
mining as has-beens or also-rans at the turn of the twenty-first
century had plenty of egg all over their faces, at least until 2008.

What they failed to see was the massive consolidation that has taken place in those (centralized) industries – and the driving force of China and other emerging markets in terms of pushing demand and pricing higher for their products.

5 So, we are growth AND value investors, AND we look for 'cheapness'. But we also recognize that our *BigIdeas* may affect companies that are today regarded as pedestrian in terms of growth, and possibly even appear to be expensive based on currently appraised prospects. That is because other investors may not yet see what we see – that a new, disruptive trend may overtake these industries. This could be where, for instance, China is hoovering up a large part of the world's steel and copper supplies – and thereby changing the dynamics of the underlying industries in dramatic fashion.

Is this all a bit confusing?

Well, this is probably the hardest part of the book to follow because the financial industry has made a specialty of obfuscating the way it works – its own 'barrier to entry'. We are trying to break down that barrier, but first we've got to arm you with some of the parlance and methods of the 'industry'.

So how about if we lay down some basic principles, and emphasize those ratios and measurements that we believe you really should take account of? And why don't we give you some guidance as to what sort of numbers you should look at?

Firstly, don't worry about what an individual share price is in money terms, i.e. its nominal price.

Whether it is US$1 or US$1000, it doesn't make it any more or less 'expensive'. Share prices are simply a function of the perceived worth of the business by the stock market divided by the number of shares outstanding. So share prices in themselves have no meaning – other than for the following reason: if the share price has risen sharply recently – or fallen a lot recently – **investigate** why. If nothing appears from your investigation to indicate that you should not buy this particular company, then go ahead and do it.

But – generally speaking – it is better to buy a share that is going up (it has positive momentum) than one that is going down. Market practitioners say that trying to judge the bottom of a share price is like trying to catch a falling knife. Be careful.

Work out the **Enterprise Value** of the business. This measure means adding all the debts of the company (and if you have a head for figures look for so-called off-balance-sheet debt) in their accounts.

Then add those debts to the so-called Market Capitalization of the company – this is the number of shares in issue ('outstanding') times the share price.

So, if the company's debt is US$100 million, and it has US$10 million shares in issue each trading at US$ 10, it has an Enterprise Value of US$100 million (its debt) plus US$100 million (its market capitalization) = US$200 million.

It is important to recognize, therefore, that these shares are not as 'cheap' as they first might appear to be.

That's because debt has to be repaid and it generally has to be repaid before the shareholders get anything.

If we get back to Stocks 101, we will remember that the value of a share is defined as the future earnings of the company and its dividends along the way. But of course that is AFTER debt has been repaid.

Furthermore, companies with debt tend to have interest to pay – impairing earnings. In a weakening economic environment, debt has proved to be the wave that has sunk many a corporate ship.

So **watch out** for debt. As a general guide, what we look for in a company (which doesn't really apply to business with lots of real estate assets, for instance) is a debt-to-equity ratio of less than 0.25/1.

That means that the **total** debt of the company is less than 25 per cent of the total shareholder funds of the business.

In addition, we like companies whose CASH earnings (which are defined as net profit plus depreciation and amortization) **are five**

times as high as their interest payments – so that these businesses, barring disaster, can continue paying interest even in a difficult economic environment.

Now let's look at two other measures: the **price to earnings ratio** and the **earnings growth** of the company.

Generally, we like it if a company's GROWTH rate of so-called earnings per share (the net income of a business divided by the number of shares outstanding), is at least 1.25 times the so-called Price Earnings Ratio of its shares.

Forecasting growth is difficult, but we are assuming that because we are investing in businesses based on a *BigIdea*, that our companies are going to grow mightily. After all, we've really thought about what we are investing in.

So let's look at a specific example:

Jim and Al really like **solar power** as a *BigIdea*.

We like the fact that it's green, it's saleable, it has got government encouragement in many countries and, most importantly, its market is expanding because its price is coming down.

Quite soon – we think in five years or so – various types of solar power will be cheaper than fossil fuel-generated power without those entirely nasty climate-changing carbon emissions.

Great stuff.

So let's assume, that by diligent research – using company reports (available for free from all listed companies' websites under 'investor relations'), the Internet (chat rooms, Google), etc. – we have identified a really good business whose shares we want to invest in.

We think that the company has it all – good management, it's in a hot (sorry about the pun) area and it's got a great technology.

We think the company can grow its earnings by 30 per cent a year for each of the next five years. That's a tall order – it carries significant execution risk – but we really think these guys can do it.

The company has NO DEBT (even better), so its enterprise value is the same as its market capitalization, and it had earnings per share in the most recent period of US$ 1 per share. The share price is US$20, so the price to earnings ratio is 20.

Therefore its growth is 30 per cent and its PE ratio is 20. That means that the ratio of growth to PE is 1.5 to 1 – and that ticks an important box for us.

The company is growing fast, so it needs all the cash it can get to buy new equipment. As a result, there is no dividend, but then, we wouldn't expect one.

Dividends will come later when the company is more MATURE and the share price is – we hope – much, much higher.

This looks like a corker and we'd buy it for our portfolio.

But we have another *BigIdea*. We like the look of copper as a metal and we have identified a tremendous copper mine in China. Management looks good and is well-recommended. But the company isn't making any money because the mine isn't yet in production.

How do we value this one?

We have to look **further out** into the future for this particular stock. The mine, we assume, WILL come into production; we believe that in two or three years time the price of copper will be much higher and that production costs won't have gone up by all that much.

So we do some analysis of how we see the company's earnings, based on all the information we can glean about the company's reserves, mining throughput, costs, taxes, etc. It's all a bit complicated but we judge the effort to be worthwhile.

And boy, are we excited. (Yes, we should probably get out more often.)

We're excited because we think that in three years' time this copper mining company will be making more money on an annual basis than its entire current market capitalization.

And even if we add on the debt of the company to the market capitalization, the figures look terrific.

So our *BigIdea* is suggesting that because copper prices are going to be much higher, because this mine will be a big money-spinner and because the shares are cheap – we buy.

It's a different way of looking at growth and value. And it's one that we believe works.

Opportunities abound as we update this book in early 2009. There are so many companies with good prospects selling at fractions of their true value, in our opinion, that investors are spoiled for choice. There are companies selling at less than their cash holdings, at huge discounts to asset values, at low PE ratios and where their business models work in almost any environment. Get out there and choose. We honestly don't think there will be a better time in our lifetimes to buy stocks of quality.

Chapter*Five*

Bonds and Cash

Bonds and cash – at the very mention of these investment classes, readers might already be suppressing yawns of boredom and thinking of turning to the next chapter.

Please don't, however.

The global economic turmoil which commenced in 2008 should have persuaded all investors that cash and debt instruments form a vital part of any portfolio. In fact, it was the absence of cash for many investors that resulted in huge write-downs in their net wealth and, in quite a few cases – financial wipe-out.

Bonds and cash can be an important part of your financial future and, believe us, they are not as boring as they may first appear. The appropriate allocation of cash to different currencies, across different banks and at differing dates of maturity in terms of deposit, can make a HUGE difference to your eventual financial outcomes.

Similarly bonds, ranging from those issued by governments to low grade so-called 'junk bonds', can have an equally positive or negative outcome on your portfolio.

When we first published this book in early 2008, our preferred currency was the Japanese yen. We are pleased to say that during 2008 this has outperformed every other currency in the world, including the newly renascent US dollar.

In this section we will update that advice and also our advice on government bonds and other bonds.

Currencies and bonds are dynamic instruments and active investors should subscribe to our newsletter to be found on our website www.wakeupnewsletter.com for periodical updates.

Everyone knows what cash is and most people know what bonds are. But both come in a dizzying array of forms and they have the capacity to make you or lose you a lot of money.

So let's start with discussing cash …

1 Cash is an important tool in building your fortune. It is the most 'liquid' – that is, saleable at short notice – of all our investment categories. When you have spare money and none of the other classes are of investment appeal – whether it's because they are too expensive or because market conditions are adverse – cash is your refuge. In 2008 there were literally millions of investors who wished that they had held onto more cash. The old motto 'cash is king' became the mantra of the year. We are at a juncture, however, where cash may not be so attractive and we will elaborate on this a little later.

2 Cash can be deployed in several ways. There are various deposits you can make and these tend to have different 'maturities', that is, the length of time for which you contract to leave your cash in a type of deposit. These deposits will typically (but not always) attract interest rates at a higher level the longer their duration. We will explain later why that is the case.

3 You can keep your cash in a variety of ways: notes and coins (which attract no interest but which you can keep nearby), and bank or other savings institutions' deposits of varying 'maturities', including instant access accounts which allow you to take your money out straight away. And, of course, you can keep your cash in a variety of currencies – anything from the Japanese yen to the South African rand. Please believe us: the currency which you keep your money in can make a BIG difference to your eventual financial outcome. Note for instance, the differing performances between the Japanese yen, the pound sterling and the Australian dollar during 2008.

4 Where you put your cash is also important – in terms of the maturity of the account, the currency of the cash, and the qual-

ity and type of financial institution. Where you hide your cash at home can also be important. Please think about all of those people who lost money in failed banks in 2008 and it becomes apparent just how important this choice is. When interest rates seem just too good to be true, they probably are. As an example, the failure of the Icelandic banks has landed a large number of European depositors with king-sized headaches.

5 In this section, we will show you how to choose an institution where you can leave your cash with confidence, and we will update our recommendation as to which currencies you should consider leaving your cash in for the remainder of the global financial crisis and beyond. We will also indicate what sort of cash levels you should think of holding depending on your circumstances (and for this please refer to the *DiagnosticGrid* in Chapter Nine).

6 We will also show that despite the fact that you should always have SOME cash – in notes, in accounts and in so-called pre-paid debit cards – cash should NEVER be the main investment you make. Cash is generally a relatively poor investment over the longer term, and that is mostly because it represents an obligation on governments. These days almost all money is so-called 'fiat money', i.e. it is issued by governments without the backing of gold or other physical reserves. So anyone who accepts cash is accepting the promise of a government, which is probably a dangerous thing to do over the longer term.

We are going to do three important things in this section in relation to cash:

- Show you where to put it and for what maturities, i.e. duration of deposit
- Show you how much cash you should have to hand for given circumstances and timeframes

- Recommend a currency 'basket' for the next ten years which will likely outperform other currencies, in our opinion. This will be one of our *BigIdeas*. Our original idea back at the start of 2008 was the Japanese yen, but this has already performed so well that we are now taking the alternative 'basket' approach.

As far as bonds are concerned, these are equally important in the construction of a successful portfolio for the next ten years.

Bonds are so-called 'fixed income obligations'. They represent a financial claim against an enterprise, typically a government or a corporation, and they come in a bewildering variety of durations.

Durations are the dates on which the bonds have to be repaid by the borrowing institution. They also carry differing yields (the amount per bond that the borrower has to pay in interest annually). That interest can be paid semi-annually, annually, or even in one lump sum at the end of the duration of the bond.

The 'starting' yield of the bond is the yield at which it is priced when first sold to investors.

Most bonds, although not all, will then 'trade' on markets, and the yields will then vary according to how the price of the bond moves in those trades. We will explain how this happens later in this section.

Bonds are a form of debt for the companies or governments that issue them. They are graded by RATING AGENCIES according to their perceived relative risk; in other words, the ability of the borrowers to repay the debt.

These ratings are important to investors, although certainly not infallible. Rating agencies have got it wrong in the past (Enron is a good example and, more recently, the likes of AIG and Lehman Brothers have had their bonds hugely over-rated by the agencies). However, these ratings are important guides. The main rating agencies are Standard & Poor's and Moody's, and many funds sold to the public investing in bonds demand that their investments be rated by one of these two. These agencies appear to have taken their eye off the ball in respect of securitized mortgage paper (for instance the so-called sub-prime debt now seared in investors' memory); they certainly didn't see the bankruptcy of the big investment banks that have so far failed in the financial crisis. But to ignore what they say now would be foolish – it's like ignoring the police just because they have made some past mistakes. So although investors should not solely consider the views of the rating agencies, they should certainly take good account of them in their investment considerations.

The problem with the earlier over-reliance by many investors on the views of rating agencies was twofold: first, there has been a huge increase in the amount of bond 'paper' issued in recent years, particularly of the 'structured' sort (the complex stuff involving securitization of mortgages, etc.) put together for the most part by investment banks for large profits. These were the famous bits of paper that turned 'toxic' and heralded our current financial crisis.

Second, the ratings agencies were typically paid for their services, not by the investors in the bonds, but by the issuers, including the large investment banks. This created an obvious potential conflict of interest.

Nonetheless, the rating of a bond can have a huge effect on its yield. Depending on their ratings, bonds offer higher or lower yields – that is, the amount of interest to be paid to the bondholder divided into the price of the bond.

Typically, a riskier bond (one with a lesser rating than a 'higher quality' bond) will yield more than a blue-chip (or cast-iron quality bond). These blue-chip bonds are issued by borrowers whose creditworthiness is perceived to be impeccable – the world's leading governments, for instance, the supranational agencies such as the World Bank, and the largest corporations with the strongest balance sheets. These would typically be rated as 'AAA' (or 'triple A') bonds.

The ratings ascribed to bonds, and by inference to the companies and governments that issue them, are very important to those institutions because they largely determine the amount they have to pay lenders to borrow their money.

Typically, a so-called straight bond (one without any fancy permutations, some of which we will cover later) is simple in concept.

It is a bit of paper (although, like shares, they are typically electronically registered now) that states the borrower (say, company X) will repay the FACE VALUE of the bond on a due date sometime in the future.

This due date can be anywhere from one month (so-called money market instruments or T-Bills) to 50 years. These straight bonds carry a 'coupon' which is the interest rate that they pay to borrowers. In the case of very short-dated bonds, this is typically reflected in the price at which the bond is to be eventually repurchased.

So, for instance, a one-month money market instrument might be issued at 100 and bought back at 100.5 in a month's time, the 0.5 being the interest that has 'accrued' on the debt over the period.

A longer-dated straight bond will pay interest, typically every six months or annually, to its holders. In some cases, such as with so-called zero coupon bonds, the interest is 'rolled up' and added to the eventual redemption price of the bond, in other words the price at which the bond is redeemed or 'paid back' at the end of its term or 'maturity'.

Governments around the world regularly issue bonds to finance their activities that cannot be met out of taxation or other sources of income. The developed world economies are, for the most part, big issuers of bonds, or at least have been in the past. For many governments, bonds are also a vital instrument of monetary policy and are used to control the supply of credit in an economy.

This is not something that needs to concern us at the moment, but it is important to note that the range of government bonds in issue is simply staggering, and the volumes traded in these bonds are extraordinarily high.

There are also all sorts of sub-government bonds; for instance US municipalities can issue their own bonds (so-called 'Munis' which can carry tax advantages for US citizens). There are also, in many countries, state and provincial bonds, as well as city bonds. There are also supranational organizational bonds (e.g. World Bank bonds) and bonds backed by government guarantees (e.g. for rail networks or for housing loans). Many of these bonds are pitched to investors with specific tax advantages.

Then there are corporate bonds – so many that it would take a library of books to list them all – and all of their various permutations.

Typically, companies issue bonds because they can raise money more cheaply by doing so than by borrowing from a bank. Also, bonds tend to be for a longer duration than a bank loan, so a company can work out more easily what the 'cost of its capital' is; i.e. the interest it has to pay over a period of time, without worrying about interest rate changes which can affect the rate paid on bank debt.

Also, companies can do fancy things when they issue bonds. For instance, they can sell what are called 'convertible bonds'. These are bonds which the borrower can convert into shares of the company at various times, rather than getting paid back in cash. This gives the bondholder two rights: one is to an income stream from the 'coupon' on the bond, as well as the right to be paid back in cash if the company's shares don't perform to plan (and also because they are bond holders, convertible owners tend to have greater rights than common shareholders); the second is convertible bond shareholders have the right if they choose to convert the bonds into the company's shares.

Put simply, a typical convertible bond will allow the bond holder to convert the value of their bond into the issuer's shares at a fixed price for a period of time, so if the shares of the company go up way beyond that fixed price, it will typically make a lot of sense for the holder to 'convert' the bond into shares.

For the company that issues them, convertible bonds carry several benefits.

A typical one is that because they can be converted into common shares, the company will tend to pay less interest on its bonds, because the bondholder is getting something 'extra'. Also, if the bondholders convert into shares, the company no longer has to redeem its bonds for cash, saving the 'repayment of the principal'. In other words the debt will have been extinguished.

Convertible bonds, therefore, can be mutually beneficial to both investors and companies. If one of the companies relating to a *Big-Idea* that you have or that you read about in this book has issued or is issuing convertible bonds, it might be a good idea to check them out.

There are ways of knowing whether a convertible bond is a good buy or not and we will provide some simple rules in respect of this at the end of this chapter.

Just to make life more complicated, there are lots of other permutations of bonds issued by companies: bonds with warrants attached (where the warrants allow the holder to buy shares at a fixed price), bonds which have certain specific security (i.e. they are not just secured against the assets of the whole company, as is typical of most bonds, but against some specific income stream or asset), etc.

In truth, most of these permutations are of no interest to the individual investor, partly because the bonds tend to be sold exclusively to institutions and are not generally readily accessible to smaller investors; and partly because the arcane nature of these instruments would demand too much attention and deflect us from our simple theme which is to preserve and enhance capital by pursing a disciplined investment approach based on the *BigIdea* strategy.

There are books on the subject if investors do want to take it further – bonds are fascinating and definitely an area worth exploring – but let us now turn to practicalities. Having gone through the types of bonds and of cash alternatives available to investors building a long-term portfolio, what do we specifically recommend?

When this book was first published at the start of 2008, our opinion was that, generally speaking, bonds around the world were more or less priced to perfection. In other words, the yield-spread (the difference in yields) between good quality blue-chip bonds and lower-grade bonds was not sufficiently high to compensate investors for the risks of default. This has proved to be correct – and in spades. The blowout in spreads has been incredible. Government bonds in major economies (not developing economies, where the opposite has occurred) have soared in price. Meanwhile corporate bonds, bonds of municipalities and of minor nations have fallen in price precipitously, which has made for the biggest ever spreads between so-called low risk bonds (e.g. US or UK government bonds) and other types of bonds.

This is because investors have sought 'safe havens' for their money at a time of economic crisis. Indeed on one particular day, US T-Bills sold for a zero rate of return – unprecedented in history.

This is despite the fact that the Anglo-Saxon governments are issuing record amounts of bonds as they seek to pay for ballooning deficits brought on by the profligacy of their governments and the failure of large swathes of their financial systems. This is counter-intuitive, but has happened in periods of great financial stress before, although not to the same extent.

In Japan, interest rates have continued to decline over the past 20 years with very long-term government bonds yielding not much more than 1 per cent, reflecting deflationary conditions and an absence of alternative investments.

For investors in US and UK bonds, however, the situation is in our opinion very different.

First of all, the recovery of their economies is likely to be much faster than the Japanese one because the policy responses of governments to the current crisis have been much more rapid than in Japan. We expect, as we say elsewhere, that the deflationary headlines will abate sometime in 2010 and inflation will start appearing. At this stage US and UK, as well as European government bonds, will look like very bad investments indeed.

The volume of government bond issuance in the current crisis will be of such a tsunami-like scale that governments will have no option but to create inflation to reduce the effect of the burden of bond repayment by effectively debauching the value of fiat or paper money.

Furthermore, because of risk aversion by insurance companies and other institutions, yields themselves on even the safest bonds do not take into account potential inflationary risks and even, dare we say it, blue-chip and governmental default or partial default risk, over the coming years.

For this reason, our broad recommendation has now changed. We believe that investors should become much more wary of government bonds and start to look at the bonds of companies which are likely to survive under almost any circumstances and which now – because of the blowout on 'spreads' – are relatively speaking much more attractive.

The cheapest and most liquid way to invest in corporate bonds is through an ETF. We suggest readers consider the iShares Sterling Corporate Bond Fund (listed in London, symbol SLXX). There is no initial fee, the expense ratio is only 0.2 per cent and at the time of writing (January 2009), it offered a yield of 8 per cent. For those interested in US dollar-denominated bonds, there is the iShares iBoxx Corporate Bond Fund (listed in New York, symbol HYG), which has an expense ratio of 0.5 per cent and yielded 11 per cent at the time of writing this.

The Bear Stearns Moment: A Watershed for Bonds and Credit – the Assassination of the Financial Archduke

When this book was first published, some serious cracks were already emerging in the long halcyon period that bond investors had enjoyed in recent years. In mid-2007, two highly leveraged funds managed by Bear Stearns got into trouble, presaging the beginnings of the end of a benign period for so-called 'junk' or low-rated debt.

These funds, known as the Enhanced Leverage Fund and the High-Grade Fund (a misnomer if there ever was one), were wiped out in all but name – even though Bear Stearns put in US$1.6 billion of its own money to try to shore them up. Then one of Europe's banks, BNP Paribas, followed with its own multi-billion-dollar fund disaster. The dominos had started to tumble. This then led on to the outright failure and takeover of Bear Stearns, the failure of Lehman Brothers, Northern Rock, the part nationalization of many banks around the world – and the biggest financial story of the post-war period.

What went wrong? Well, these Bear Stearns funds had four things going against them: first, in a rising interest-rate environment investing in so-called 'collateralized debt obligations' linked to sub-prime mortgages wasn't a great idea; second, borrowing on top of those already-risky investments wasn't bright-spark stuff either; third, investors demanded their money back; and fourth, other banks – sensing blood – began to make 'margin' calls or emergency cash calls. Not a pretty picture.

All of this happened just as everything seemed great, the garden for bond investors was rosy, and yields hovered at low levels. When all seems too good to be true, it generally is.

Indeed, in the preceding year (2006), the default rate (i.e. the failure to pay either interest or principal on the part of the borrower) on so-called 'high-yield' (i.e. junk, or non-investment grade) investments was the lowest for 25 years.

But strains in the US housing market started to alter this – and it is now evident that the Bear Stearns funds debacle represented a kind of fatal turning point for the merry game played in bond markets in the past 20 or so years.

The Bear Stearns funds specialized in investing in the most exotic segments of 'sub-prime' mortgage paper, i.e. basically mortgages where the credit quality of the individuals taking them out was the poorest in the market. In some cases, no credit checks were undertaken at all on these types of mortgages, which often were advanced against the full (i.e. 100 per cent) value of the properties backing them.

Because the sub-prime US mortgage market started running into trouble in early 2007, it was only a matter of time before the funds that 'played' in them also experienced difficulties. Bear Stearns not only took on the riskiest kinds of loans for their funds, but they also borrowed on top of them to add extra risk.

As US interest rates started to go up, these and other types of incendiary bond-related investments began to be exposed for what they were: dangerous.

The huge explosion in the private equity field, and particularly in the buy-out area, was a major contributory factor in the growth of lesser-quality bond debt in world markets. This abundance of second-rate debt had been enhanced by a culture of 'easy money' policies pursued by many of the central banks of major economies.

This has meant that credit growth generally outpaced economic growth, which led to systemic over-borrowing. In these circumstances, one day the chickens will always come home to roost, and the inflection point for these chickens was sometime mid-2007.

We warned of these factors in our previous book, *Wake Up!* – and now, for many bond investors, that warning came perilously true.

In the first publication of this book, we generally believed that investors should stay away from corporate and other forms of lesser quality bonds because of the huge risks associated with the 'easy money' period that looked to us to be coming to an end.

We also indicated that we thought that the most interesting long bonds for our readers to monitor were those of the US government at the so-called 'long' end (30-year Treasury bonds) and those of the Japanese government (called JGBs) of ten years' duration. We gave some price points on these that were not directly reached. Nonetheless, these have been by far the best investments in the bond universe since the book was published.

It is now time to take a contrary view.

Our new, updated view is that Anglo-Saxon government bonds represent poor value and are likely to decline in price.

Some corporate bonds (those of what we call 'proxy governments' such as huge companies like BP andUnilever) represent much better value than government bonds. Bonds of these companies are liquid (i.e. easy to buy and sell) and brokers can advise on which are the best to buy.

We also remain positive on certain types of convertible bonds, which are detailed below.

However, overall we think that investors should look out for significant falls in developed government bond prices at some time in the next few years.

Some reasons why bond prices in general might fall sharply could be as follows.

The US is heavily indebted to foreigners. If, as we expect, the US dollar resumes its long-term devaluation in response to trade deficits and to a move to diversify foreign exchange reserves away from US dollars by the major Asian central banks, then bond yields in the US could expand.

This would be because the US could be forced to raise interest rates to defend a plunging currency. This is counterintuitive to what is happening at the moment, when investors are seeking safe havens for their money and paying almost any price for the debts of major economies.

At the right PRICE and at the RIGHT exchange rates, US government bonds would be an attractive proposition, but that price is much lower than today's levels. Keep a watching brief and follow our newsletter for updates.

We also mentioned in the earlier edition of this book that the euro was a sell against the dollar at a rate of €1 = US$1.55. As it happened, it reached a level of US$1.60 = €1 in the summer of 2008.

It is now, at the time of publication, about €1.30 = US$1, so that has worked out as a good sale. Our view currently is that the US dollar **and** the euro are both vulnerable, for similar as well as different reasons, to falls against other currencies.

In the case of the euro, it is because it is fundamentally overvalued and countries such as France, Italy and Spain cannot compete internationally in export markets at these levels of the exchange rate.

For that reason the euro is likely to fall further against the US dollar and other currencies – but the US dollar will have its own issues which will soon become evident.

The ultimate debauching of the US currency by the excessive creation of new paper will lead in time to the US dollar falling against just about EVERY currency and the main currency recommendation of this section is to get OUT of US dollars. The printing presses have been and are running hot in the United States, and while the velocity (or circulation) of money remains low, a simple spark of confidence will set the US off an inflationary course that it both desires and needs to reduce its external indebtedness. This will be accompanied by a fall in the US dollar against almost everything. The recent rallies in the US dollar, which we heralded in the first edition of this book, provide an excellent opportunity to sell the currency.

In the case of the pound sterling, we recommended selling the currency as it approached £2.20 to the US dollar. *It got very near to there.* At that level, we stated that the UK economy would be deeply uncompetitive and the pound grossly overvalued – therefore it would be time to sell. Sure enough, the pound fell precipitously through the winter of 2008 and is now, in our opinion, undervalued against the dollar. The headlines of pessimism about the UK economy are so universal as to cause us to pause for thought – and indeed we think that at about US$1.45 to £1, the pound should be a buy.

We are not saying that the UK economy is in a great shape – it isn't. But relative to the US and to the euro zone, it may have advantages. One of these is its flexibility, and the rapid response of its exchange rate in adjusting to the external and internal pressures of the economy. In our view, the long-term value of the euro and of the dollar is more perilous than that of the pound.

The UK's public debt stands at around 44 per cent of GDP, making it the lowest of the G7 countries. The most indebted G7 nation as a percentage of its GDP is Japan (170 per cent) followed by Italy (104 per cent). US public debt stands at around 61 per cent of GDP. We believe that Britain's Conservative Party will win the next election and this will result in a return to balanced budgets and tax cuts over time.

We can't say the same for the euro zone which is run by many governments yet by one central bank.

The whole of the so-called euro zone is vulnerable to what Leuven University's Professor Paul de Grauwe calls 'asymmetric shocks'. All of the euro zone countries pursue differing wage policies and these lead to divergent trends.

The problem for the euro is more complex than that for sterling; there are 21 countries that use the euro as their currency (including the likes of Monaco, the Vatican City and San Marino) – and all of them move at different speeds. In recent years, Germany has been squeezing wage costs through improved productivity; Ireland and Spain enjoyed booms which proved unsustainable; and France and Italy have got themselves into big messes.

Now that a serious recession has developed in several of these key countries, this is beginning to put an intolerable strain on the monetary union. It is why we do not recommend the euro as anything other than a shorter-term 'punt' (or gamble) for investors.

Within the euro zone the only 'safe' economies are Holland, Germany, Luxembourg and, possibly, Belgium. In general, the higher the euro goes against other major currencies, the worse the other economies of the euro zone will be in terms of potential crisis and, for this reason, we generally recommend that investors currently avoid euro-denominated investments in countries such as Greece, Italy, France, Portugal, Spain and Ireland. Some of these countries would be better off leaving the euro and reverting to their former currencies to allow them to devalue and establish a competitive exchange rate. For instance, Italy's unit labour costs are 40 per cent higher today than in 1995. Unfortunately, such a move is likely to be too politically sensitive and thus unlikely to happen. But in the long term, it would be better for the euro as well as these ailing, uncompetitive economies.

So, if investors are thinking about bonds in the construction of their portfolios, we have the following two points for you to consider:

First, sell US and UK government bonds, particularly long dated ones.

For your cash holdings, we recommend that you hold at least 30 per cent of your cash deposits in your base currency, i.e. the currency used where you live or where your greatest outgoings are. For the remaining 70 per cent, create a basket of up to four additional currencies from the following list (obviously exclude your base currency if it is in this list): UK pounds, Japanese yen, Australian dollars, Canadian dollars, Swiss francs and Brazilian real. Do not allocate more than 20 per cent to any one currency.

For example, if you live in the UK, your currency basket may look like this: 30 per cent UK pounds, 20 per cent Swiss francs, 20 per cent Australian dollars, 15 per cent Japanese yen and 15 per cent Canadian dollars.

Secondly, we would avoid euros at current levels and also the US dollar. Please feel free to visit our website for up-to-the-moment reviews of these recommendations.

US government bonds are to be avoided until the US dollar has run the full course of its fall against other currencies, and this could take some time. We believe that over the next five years, the US dollar could fall 30 per cent against a basket of other major currencies. In addition, if your search for *BigIdeas* throws up companies which have convertible bonds in issue which are readily accessible to private investors, we do recommend that you consult a stockbroker, but it may be worthwhile buying those convertibles as a safer way of investing in that business.

We offer below some tips on exactly what sort of parameters you might want to look at before investing in a convertible bond.

1. The bond should have preferential status in the event of a corporate liquidation to common equity (or ordinary shares). This means that you stand a better chance of getting something back if the company goes bust.

2. The convertible bond should carry a 'coupon' or interest payment higher than the yield on the company's ordinary shares; so for instance if SOLAR Limited (a mythical company) issues a convertible bond at a 4 per cent annual 'coupon' but its ordinary shares' dividend yield (the dividend payment annually divided by the share price currently prevailing) is less than 4 per cent, then that particular box can be positively ticked.

3. The convertible bond should allow you to convert into the company's shares at a 'premium' to the share price that is not too great to the current prevailing share price. So for instance, if the share price is $10, and the price at which you can 'convert' your bonds is $12.50, the premium will be 25 per cent. Generally, we don't like convertible bonds that have a premium of more than 25 per cent because it means that there is a high hurdle for the shares to reach before it becomes worthwhile for bond holders to convert to becoming shareholders.

4. The terms of the timing of conversion should be straightforward, as should be the method. In other words, if you want to convert because the share price has gone above the level at which it becomes worthwhile, it should be easy for you or your stockbroker to do so. Here, professional advice from a stockbroker would be invaluable as sometimes these conversion terms can be arcane.

But in principle we like convertible bonds as a class. They offer some downside protection in the form of better security over the assets of the company than a straightforward investment in shares. They also typically have a yield which is superior to the yield on common shares and they offer convertibility into shares if the share price rises, so they also have the prevailing feature of being potentially common or ordinary shares.

However, investors should not simply invest in a convertible bond because it is available. Many companies haven't issued them and if the only way for you to take advantage of one of your own *BigIdeas* is to invest in ordinary shares, then so be it. But 'converts' can be a neat way of making an investment into a company that you like the look of.

As far as **cash** is concerned, we believe that the paramount issue for investors should be safety and also the deployment of your cash in the best positioned currencies.

Most people live in one place. So for most readers of this book, one currency will be the most important in their lives. It's pretty evident that, in our everyday life, we will need our local currency for spending purposes. Unless you live in a banana republic, where rampant inflation prevails (say Zimbabwe), then your local currency will tend to be RELATIVELY stable.

Because all of us should aim to match our assets and our liabilities in life, we should keep some emergency reserves in our 'home' currency.

These reserves should be kept in banks with strong credit (and even then, spread around so as to take maximum advantage of various government depositor protection schemes), or in money market funds or such which have equivalent ratings. Cash in itself tends to be a poor performer over time; it is eroded in purchasing power by inflation, and rarely does it generate real returns after tax for prolonged periods.

So cash in your 'home' currency should be limited to the following:

1 As a reserve for emergencies, you should keep, at home, in notes, about a three months' supply of spending money.

2 As a reserve for other emergencies and as a contingency, you should keep about six months' worth of cash in your bank – in an account that pays interest. Don't shop around too much on the interest rate for this particular cash hoard – typically higher rates of interest carry higher degrees of risk, and you really shouldn't take any risk with your contingency cash.

3 As a strategic reserve – in other words, as a long-term hedge against the possible decline of your own currency and as a way of holding funds when you are not fully invested – consider a foreign currency.

BigIdea # 5

Investing in the Japanese yen WAS our *BigIdea* number 5.

The problem is that since the book was first published, the yen has risen by about 25 per cent against the dollar, and over 40 per cent against the pound. It is now no longer as attractive as it was then.

So our *BigIdea* number 5 now is – sell the US dollar against almost anything. In another section, we talk about gold as a great idea, and that is one of the substitutes; but we also now like commodity proxies which have been very badly beaten up, such as the Canadian dollar and the Australian dollar.

And because we don't think the fundamentals of the UK economy are as bad as many do – and we believe that there will be a positive change of government – the pound is a buy against the US dollar also.

Of course, there are more exotic currencies that may appreciate even further, for instance, the Chinese Yuan, but these are difficult for foreigners to buy and are, in any case, a little riskier.

BigIdea # 6

On the subject of cash, consider this: when you travel and use credit cards, or even when you carry cash, you are subject to all sorts of risks – theft and fraud amongst them.

So we bring you our next *BigIdea*: the prepaid debit card. Issued by an 'offshore' bank, it is a good alternative to carrying cash around. These prepaid debit cards function just as ordinary debit or credit cards do: they can be used at ATMs around the world, and used in stores, restaurants, etc.

But they carry a finite ('pre-loaded') amount of money – in most major currencies – and they carry relatively low transaction fees. Furthermore, they can be 'topped up' on the internet and be made to look like business or ID cards.

They are the modern equivalent of travellers' cheques – anonymous, portable and relatively safe.

In the United States, many banks issue prepaid debit cards to US citizens, and indeed there are an estimated 300 million now in circulation, many of them gift cards.

This *BigIdea* was, in fact, directly prompted by the review of bonds and cash undertaken in this section.

Money and its transmission is a huge international business – think of the literally billions of dollars or equivalent that whizz around the international banking system on a daily basis. Furthermore, each of us regularly spends money in shops, bars and restaurants using credit cards, debit cards, cheques or cash.

All of these payments systems have evolved over time (in our book, *Wake Up!*, we describe the development of money over the millennia) but it is only relatively recently, in the past 50 years or so, that plastic payment solutions, led by the ubiquitous credit card, have come to the fore.

These payment solutions use a highly sophisticated network of banks, processors and umbrella organizations (such as MasterCard,

Visa and American Express) to facilitate transactions internationally and on a vast scale.

These 'plastic' based ways of paying will increasingly be supplanted by surrogates – not necessarily replacing the existing organizations that move money and credit around, but by employing different methods of transmission.

For instance, the use of mobile phones to pay bills will become increasingly prominent. In Japan and elsewhere in Asia, many small transactions are accomplished by putting a mobile phone into a cradle that then deducts small amounts from an implanted chip in the mobile phone. Increasingly, mobile phones will come to be important all-in-one alternatives to carrying cash.

Apart from prepaid cards and mobile phones, a whole raft of new technologies is being developed which in time – and we believe about 20 years will be plenty in this respect – will edge out cash as the preferred way of making small transactions. And this development applies to the whole world.

The market opportunity for new methods of money transfer is phenomenally large. Beneficiaries will be companies that develop the relevant technology, companies that displace banks that currently make excess profits from their credit card businesses, and so-called 'e-wallet' and 'tap and go' payment solutions.

To give readers an idea of the scale of the opportunity:

In the UK, the prepaid debit card market is expected to grow from 2 million cards in issue today to about 44 million by 2010.

Already, trials are under way in Europe where people are having tiny data chips implanted under their skin to enable them to simply 'wave and pay'. Yes really. For the moment, we think this technology may be a step too far.

But more realistically, the use of mobile phones to pay bills will become more and more ubiquitous. 'Pay by Mobile', using cradles installed in shops and SMS/texting based systems are already prevalent in Japan.

E-payment solutions such as PayPal or Neteller, which allow users to pay quickly and securely for online purchases, will continue to grow apace.

Although traditional banks might, on the surface, seem not to be so keen on these new payment solutions developing, this is not the case. The old-style banks are, in many cases, at the vanguard of encouraging the move to a cashless society as it is very much in their interest.

This is because the cost of transferring physical cash is a high one for banks everywhere. For example, it has been estimated by McKinsey, a consultancy, that in Europe, the total cost of moving money around is about $30 billion a year, or about 8 per cent of all banks' total operational expenses. So it makes clear sense for banks to encourage the use of new and cashless payments solutions.

The fact is that over the next ten years or so the following will occur:

1 Personal cheques will become obsolete in almost every major jurisdiction.
2 Prepaid debit cards will continue to grow at a very fast rate, particularly in Europe and Asia.
3 The use of mobile phones to effect payments will explode – first, for small transactions, using 'tap and go' cradle technology (which can also be used with prepaid cards, incidentally), and second with the use of web-enabled phones to effect payments.
4 Online payment solutions – so called e-wallets – will be perfected and online transfers of money will become the major way in which money is transmitted.
5 Over time, cash will be displaced in almost every market – though its 'abolition' is at least 20 years away.

So how do we as investors benefit from this next *BigIdea* – the incontrovertible growth of the cashless society?

One way is to 'play' the growth of prepaid cards.

There are several ways in which a bank can make money out of the fast-growing prepaid debit card market.

First, there is the 'float' – that is, the money loaded onto cards but not yet spent. The interest on this, which can be considerable, belongs to the issuing bank.

Then there are the various fees – such as issuing fees, transaction fees and foreign exchange fees, which the issuing bank benefits from.

Another beneficiary of this prospective boom in prepaid cards will be the issuing networks. Visa and MasterCard, which are owned in part by member banks, are the leaders in providing the payments networks through which such cards operate.

MasterCard in particular is interesting. It is listed in the US and, although a large company, appears to us to have considerable growth ahead of it. This is a share that readers might consider as a 'safe' way of participating in the move towards a cashless society.

The second area for investors to consider in assessing corporate prospects in the move to a cashless society is in so-called Near Field Communications (NFC).

This uses a hidden embedded computer chip (in a card, a phone or your body), linked to radio frequency antennae. After the NFC-enabled device (or body) is passed at the point-of-sale, payment details are sent wirelessly to the payment scheme network. Moments after payment is initiated, confirmation is received both by the vendor and by the buyer.

As an example of this, MasterCard operates a system called Pay Pass which allows users to 'tap and go'. This is faster than cash, enabling retailers to handle more customers in less time. It is faster than a swipe, and has been found to encourage sales where, for instance, customers don't have enough ready cash on them.

But, of course, NFC can and will be used in conjunction with other delivery methods other than cards; this, for instance, can be through the mobile phone or a key fob.

One way of keeping an eye on this technology is through the website of the industry forum; most of the mobile handset manufacturers are already members of this. Look at www.nfc-forum.org to keep a general eye on industry developments.

In Japan, as of mid 2008, over 12 million units of so-called 'wallet phones' have already been shipped, with Sony as the market leader with a technology called 'Felica', where the handsets have been sold through the leading mobile company, DoCoMo.

In the US, NFC is as yet confined to limited trials on cards, and in Europe it is a year or two away from being implemented.

But make no mistake, dear reader: within a year or two, there will be a move worldwide to adopt this technology as a preferred form of payment. With over 500 million mobile phones sold worldwide every year, and with developing economy usage of mobile technology fast catching up with that of the developed world – this technology will be EVERYWHERE.

And soon, this technology will morph into a world in which we have fully integrated mobile payment solutions. This, in our opinion, is by far the best opportunity for future payment solutions as an area for investment.

This solution literally provides an 'e-wallet' – a means of carrying 'electronic cash' with you wherever you go. The main difference between this and all previous technology is that the mobile phone is actually the payment delivery system itself.

The key feature of this is that the payment facility is one directly linked to the retailer, bypassing the payment network infrastructure (e.g. banks, MasterCard and Visa), thereby saving on what are known as 'interchange fees'.

One company that is a leader in this field is C-SAM, based in Chicago in the US. See www.c-sam.com for updated information. This company was one of the first to see the benefits of convergence between mobile and payments technology.

Early on, C-SAM viewed money transfer, bill payments, prepaid phone cards, person-to-person transactions and stored cash applications as key entry points to the mobile commerce market and developed products for each of these. Now it and a number of other companies are ready to bring genuine 'cashless' technology to the world of everyday transactions.

C-SAM uses a product called OneWallet, which replaces all physical cards, letting users conduct all their payments through their phones or the web. It is complex in terms of system implementation but is simple for the user; it is also a 'white label' product, enabling existing card or retail companies to retain their customers with 'virtual' cards.

The companies to watch in this dynamic and exciting area are:

1 **Neovia Financial**, a UK-listed company. This company has a good chance of becoming a market leader in prepaid debit, then, subsequently, in NFC cards in Europe, creating large upside potential.

2 **C-SAM**. This company is not listed, but may be one day. Readers should check its website for regular updates on any financing that it may be undertaking (www.c-sam.com).

3 **MasterCard**. A behemoth of the industry, but with a strong market position and a potential leader in NFC-enabled cards (symbol: MA:US).

4 **Sony**. A leader in cradle and point-of-sale (POS) phone technology. The problem is that this company does a multiplicity of other things, but having a few shares of Sony, listed in Japan and in the US, will probably be no bad thing.

5 **TxtTrans Ltd**. Another unlisted company, this time one from the UK, this is a leader in banking verification systems. This is another company that readers should watch, both to observe industry trends and to see if the company does a public financing. The company's website is www.txttrans.com.

Chapter*Six*

The BRIC Economies

If you haven't already come across this relatively new and trendy word, BRIC is an acronym for Brazil, Russia, India and China. Rather conveniently, it is also a pun on the word brick, which conveys solidity, sturdiness and stability. It was first coined in 2003 in a report published by Goldman Sachs, a former investment bank, turned bank holding company. The report proposed that these four BRIC countries would become substantial players in the global economy by 2050, rivalling today's dominant economies. The following chart illustrates the projected growth from 2000 to 2050 in five year intervals. G6 countries are defined as being France, Germany, Italy, Japan, UK and US. The chart indicates that sometime between 2035 and 2040, the BRIC economies are expected to overtake those of the G6. The implications of such a bold projection will transform the global economic landscape and redistribute wealth and power.

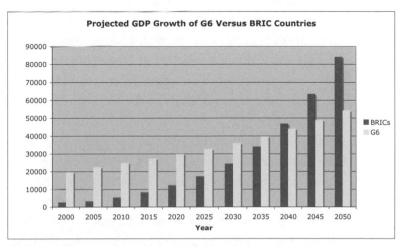

Data Source: Goldman Sachs Global Economics Paper no: 99. Dreaming with BRICs: The Path to 2050

Clearly 2008 was a disastrous year as far as stock market performance goes, and the stock markets of the BRIC economies were by no means spared. Some BRIC economy stock markets fell by half in 2008. However, it is important not to lose sight of the fact that we are taking a 10-year view – the economic rise of the BRICs is inevitable, especially China and India where GDP growth has remained at or near double digits for over a decade. We may certainly see a slowdown as a result of the global financial crisis for one or two years, but the BRICs are still on track to overtake those of the G6 by around 2035. So we remain very much pro-BRICs for the long term, regardless of the global recession for 2009 and possibly 2010 that we are facing. Volatility is the nature of emerging markets and long-term investors should not be panicked by it.

It is of course dangerous to consider the BRIC economies as one. Although they do have much in common, they have even more differences. Simply dividing your BRIC investment into four parts of 25 per cent is not necessarily the best strategy. The allocation or weighting across these countries needs careful consideration based on the future growth prospects and risk of each country over the next ten years.

Let us review each BRIC country so that you at least have a basic overview of their size, growth and prospects (data sourced from the Economist Intelligence Unit, EIU and the CIA World Factbook).

Translating these numbers into an overall picture of the country's prospects, **Brazil** is a large country with a young workforce, experiencing steady population growth. Its real growth rate, though, is more that of a developed country, i.e. below 5 per cent, than that of an emerging one. It has a strong reliance on the United States for its exports and is a net exporter.

Brazil needs to implement deeper reforms if it is going to increase and sustain its GDP growth, but this appears to be too challenging for the current government. A lack of reforms will stifle future growth – that, we believe, is the greatest challenge Brazil's economy is facing.

Although the largest country by landmass, **Russia** has a relatively small population. The demographics do not look good over the long-term; the work force's average age is in the late 30s and the population

Brazil – Fast Facts

Population: 196.4 million (world's fifth largest)
Median Age: 28.3 years
Population Growth: 1.2%
2007 GDP: US$1.31 trillion
Real GDP Growth: 3.6% (2003–2007 average)
Inflation: 4.2% (2003–2007 average)
Exports/Imports (2007 est.): $160 billion/$120 billion ($40 billion trade surplus)
Top 3 Export Partners: United States (16.1%), Argentina (9.2%), China (6.8%)
Foreign Exchange Reserves: $180 billion (31 December 2007)
Public Debt: 45.1% of GDP (2007 est.)

Russia – Fast Facts

Population: 140.7 million (world's ninth largest)
Median Age: 38.3 years
Population Growth: 0.5%
2007 GDP: US$1.29 trillion
Real GDP Growth: 7.3% (2003–2007 average)
Inflation: 11.2% (2003–2007 average)
Exports/Imports (2007 est.): $355.5 billion/$223.4 billion ($132.1 billion trade surplus)
Top 3 Export Partners: Netherlands (12.2%), Italy (7.8%), Germany (7.5%)
Foreign Exchange Reserves: $476.4 billion (31 December 2007 est.)
Public Debt: 5.9% of GDP (2007 est.)

is steadily declining. Its inflation rate, which is in double digits, doesn't look too healthy, although this is likely to fall until energy prices recover. Almost two-thirds of its exports are oil- and gas-related, so its future economic success is too directly linked to high oil and gas prices. Russia sits on around 25 per cent of the world's gas reserves.

The murder of former Federal Security Serviceman, Alexander Litvinenko, in London in November 2006 sparked renewed suspicions about Russia reverting to its covert KGB days of the Cold War. Additionally, the US-led missile shield plan to install surface-to-air missiles in Europe to protect against rogue state attacks has aggravated Russia.

Russia's invasion of (and subsequent withdrawal from) Georgia in 2008 over South Ossetia served to reinforce the West's view that Russia is reverting to its expansionist, Soviet-style ways.

Political tensions with the West, as well as armed conflict with neighbouring states such as the Ukraine and Georgia, are the greatest risk to investing in Russia. Offsetting this risk is energy-hungry and cash-rich China, a nation that is more than happy to buy Russia's oil and gas should the West take steps to reduce its reliance on Russian energy.

India – Fast Facts

Population: 1.15 billion (world's second largest)
Median Age: 25.1 years
Population Growth: 1.6%
2007 GDP: US$1.1 trillion
Real GDP Growth: 8.9% (2003–2007 average)
Inflation: 4.9% (2003–2007 average)
Exports/Imports (2007 est.): $151.3 billion/$230.5 billion ($79.2 billion trade deficit)
Top 3 Export Partners: United States (15%), China (8.7%), United Arab Emirates (8.7%)
Foreign Exchange Reserves: $275 billion (31 December 2007 est.)
Public Debt: 58.2% of GDP (2007 est.)

India's population is second only to China. It has a very young workforce and a healthy population growth. It is incredibly reliant on imports for its petroleum (which makes up almost a third of its total imports). Although it has reasonable exports, it is running a trade deficit, i.e. it imports more goods and services than it exports. Domestic consumption is a positive sign that the population's purchasing power is increasing, but it needs to be balanced with stronger exports. In basic terms, nations grow wealthy by selling goods and services to other nations, not by buying goods and services from other nations. India's weak infrastructure threatens to put the brakes on her growth story – roads, trains, airports and telecommunications are running at well above capacity. For example, trying to get from Mumbai airport to the city centre can often take three hours by car, even though they are approximately only 20 kilometres apart. The other concern that may hold India back from its potential is the government's heel-dragging in opening up its economy and embracing free trade.

China – Fast Facts

Population: 1.33 billion (world's largest)
Median Age: 33.6 years
Population Growth: 0.6%
2007 GDP: US$3.2 trillion
Real GDP Growth: 10.8% (2003–2007 average)
Inflation: 2.6% (2003–2007 average)
Exports/Imports (2007 est.): $1.22 trillion/$905 billion ($315 billion trade surplus)
Top 3 Export Partners: United States (19.1%), Hong Kong (15.1%), Japan (8.4%)
Foreign Exchange Reserves: $1.53 trillion (31 December 2007 est.)
Public Debt: 18.4% of GDP (2007 est.)

China has been the headline story for a number of years now. After a few false starts, it appears that, this time, it's for real. It has the world's largest population with an average age of 33.6 and only a slight population growth. It also has the world's largest foreign currency reserves, reaching $2 trillion in 2008. Although its exports rival those of the US, it's the domestic consumption potential that has yet to realize its true potential – 1.3 billion consumers; a truly compelling consumer base.

So do the BRIC economies still show promise over the next ten years? Let's see how they do against the four key determinants of growth:

- **Macro-economic stability** – factors such as low inflation, a balanced budget and a sound fiscal policy are healthy indicators for stability.
- **Government/politics** – unpredictable governments are a big turn-off for foreign investors. Governments need to be open, fair, stable and be able to police, but not interfere with, the private sector.
- **Free trade** – the ideal economy would have no trade barriers, such as quotas, tariffs, export or import taxes. This is the most efficient business environment for global trade.
- **Education** – the intellectual capital of the future workforce is the key to a country's prosperity.

The table below is how we think the BRIC countries score against these four determinants of growth.

Growth Factor	BRIC Country			
	Brazil	Russia	India	China
Macro-economic stability	Fair	Poor	Good	Good
Government	Fair	Poor	Fair	Fair
Free trade	Poor	Poor	Poor	Fair
Education	Fair	Fair	Poor	Good
OVERALL RATING	Fair	Poor	Fair	Good

The clear favourite for us is China. Al has been based in Hong Kong for over 13 years and visits China frequently, and he never ceases to be fascinated by the rate of progress and development there.

Anyone flying into either Beijing or Shanghai (Pudong) for the first time cannot help but be impressed with the modernity and efficiency of these airports, on a par with any of their Western international counterparts.

All readers by now have heard of China's two major cities: Beijing (capital and host of the 2008 summer Olympics) and Shanghai (financial centre), each with a population of around 15 million. Much of the growth to date has been driven out of the three major hubs of China – Beijing in the north, Shanghai in the east and Guangdong province in the south, bordering Hong Kong. But this growth is just the tip of the iceberg. The central part of China is starting to wake up and so is the west. There are also massive economic booms under way in the north-east beyond Beijing – the growth in cities such as Tianjin, Dalian and Shenyang is startling to see – and these are not small towns we are talking about. Take a look at this list of ten cities in China with populations of over five million (the list is by no means exhaustive):

- Tianjin (over 10 million people)
- Chongqing (7 million people)
- Wuhan (9 million people)
- Hangzhou (6.5 million people)
- Dalian (6 million people)
- Chengdu (10.5 million people)
- Harbin (9.5 million)
- Guangzhou (12.5 million)
- Shenzhen (9 million)
- Nanjing (8 million)

There are many more large cities in China that are starting to gather steam. In all, China has over 100 cities with a population of over one million. To give you some kind of a reference to a western city of this size, Dallas in the US has a population of around 1.2 million and Birmingham in the UK has a population of around 1 million. It's difficult to express the sheer scale of China's economic expansion – but there is no mistaking that it's happening.

Granted, we may not see GDP growth of 10 plus per cent in 2009 and possibly 2010 due to the global financial crisis, but China's $2 trillion reserves are vast and the government has pledged a fiscal stimulus package to maintain growth and employment until the economy recovers.

Although the acronym BRIC that was introduced in 2003 by Goldman Sachs refers specifically to four countries, since that time, some analysts and investors have added a few more countries. Although the core four remain Brazil, Russia, India and China, some variations include Mexico, South Africa and/or Vietnam. The one we believe is worth mentioning for the long term is Vietnam. We're not going to try and come up with a new acronym that incorporates the V, because we can't think of one that sounds as punchy as BRIC (if only Vietnam started with a vowel). Let's just think of it as an honorary BRIC. Vietnam has a come a long way in a short time. Although it doesn't have the impressive scale of China and India, we believe its longer-term outlook is very positive. Let's take a look at some of its key economic data.

Vietnam is a quite a densely populated country. Part of the former French colony 'Indochine' or Indochina, it was ravaged by the drawn-out war with the US. But it has put all that behind it now and has focused on economic growth since the turn of the century, and there are plenty of signs that it is starting to pay off. There are two noteworthy economic milestones for Vietnam that have contributed to spurring growth: one is that it opened its first stock exchange in 2000; and the other is that it joined the World Trade Organization (WTO) in January 2007.

Vietnam – Fast Facts

Population: 86 million
Median Age: 26.9 years
Population growth: 1.0%
2006 GDP: US$70 billion
Real GDP Growth: 8.1% (2003–2007 average)
Inflation: 7.1% (2003–2007 average)
Exports/Imports (2007 est.): $48.6 billion/$58.9 billion ($10.3 billion trade deficit)
Top 3 Export Partners: United States (20.8%), Japan (12.5%), Australia (7.3%)
Foreign Exchange Reserves: $23.9 billion (31 December 2007)
Public Debt: 42% of GDP (2007 est.)

Vietnam is well-positioned geographically in Asia, neighbouring China, with a vast coastline that spans the entire eastern side of the country. It has oil reserves and produces around 400,000 barrels a day as its primary export. It also has a significant textile industry that makes up around 15 per cent of its economy. Vietnam has a young workforce and has managed almost 8 per cent GDP growth since 2002.

Unfortunately, Vietnam's economy over-heated in 2008 as a result of too much foreign money being invested into it, and inflation at one point reached 30 per cent. The global financial crisis has inevitably hurt the country's economy and its stock market was down more than 70 per cent from its highs in 2008. That said, we do remain positive about Vietnam's long-term prospects as its fundamentals are sound, especially now that all the forced sellers and speculators have exited. Once again, as with all emerging markets, there will be volatility.

BigIdea # 7

Despite the strong performance of the BRIC economies over the past few years, we saw some major corrections in 2008. As a result, we believe that investing monthly into the BRICs in 2009 is a sound long-term investment strategy, as all the bad news has now been factored into their stock markets. Remember that the BRIC economies are set to overtake those of the G6 by 2035.

We do not believe that allocating 25 per cent of your investment to each BRIC economy is the best approach. Our view is that Brazil still faces some reform problems that will hold it back somewhat; Russian politics threatens to hamper its future economic success; and India suffers from a poor business infrastructure, escalating wages and a difficult business environment that is deterring the next wave of foreign investors. Furthermore, India's trade deficit is not conducive to the country's long-term growth prospects, so this needs to be watched carefully.

We believe that there are some hot spots in China, such as Beijing and Shanghai, although they have been cooling off in 2008–09, but overall growth will continue and we will start to see this in the secondary and tertiary cities over the coming few years.

That is not to say investing in China bears any less risk than the other BRIC economies. Anyone who has been following the Chinese stock market will no doubt be aware that it has been one thrilling, turbo-charged rollercoaster ride.

Readers need to be careful when investing in China's stock market because local retail investors have become seriously addicted to it. The Chinese gambling psyche has unfortunately mistaken the stock market for Macau (the Las Vegas of Asia located in southern China). As a result, the Chinese stock market is being used by many local 'investors' (read gamblers) as a casino; in other words, for purely speculative purposes with no understanding of what the company they are investing does or how it should be valued. These investor-gamblers are average citizens with no financial knowledge and have heard about the phenomenal returns that can be achieved in the stock market. Thousands of Chinese people queue up daily to open brokerage accounts so that they can take part in the big game of investment roulette. Although many of these investor-gamblers suffered terribly as the markets fell sharply in 2008, we can still expect to see a new wave of speculators jumping in at the first signs of a recovery. Investors shouldn't get sucked into the euphoria. Think long term and invest monthly to smooth out your entry price.

Another factor to consider before investing in China is its currency; the Yuan (also called the Renminbi) is not tradable outside China (yet). A Chinese person living in China wishing to invest in the stock market only has access to the Shanghai and Shenzhen stock exchanges. These shares, which are only accessible to domestic investors, are referred to as A-shares and are listed in Shanghai and Shenzhen.

Foreign investors wishing to invest in Chinese listed companies can access them through a different category of shares known as B-shares. There is also a category of Chinese listed companies known as H-shares (sometimes referred to as red chips). These H-shares are listed in Hong Kong. For example, ICBC or Bank of China both list A-shares and H-shares in China and Hong Kong. As illogical as this may sound, the price of a company's H-shares typically trades at a discount to its A-share price, even though they are on a par with each other.

This happens because there are no arbitrage opportunities to close the gap in the price differential – foreigners cannot purchase A-shares and Chinese investors in China cannot purchase H-shares unless they have money sitting outside mainland China. This results in two separate supply/demand equilibriums of A-shares and H-shares for the same company. If we use ICBC as an example again, its H-shares have been trading at a 25 per cent discount to its A-shares. So are A-shares overvalued by 25 per cent or are H-shares undervalued by 25 per cent? The answer probably lies somewhere in the middle, so we believe that investing in H-shares is a wiser choice.

The other advantage of buying into H-shares is that they are listed on the Hong Kong stock exchange, which is better regulated and more transparent than its Chinese counterparts.

There is also a longer-term prospect of the appreciation of the Hong Kong dollar. H-shares are denominated in Hong Kong dollars which are pegged to the US dollar – actually, the relationship is called a thick peg, which means that the currency is allowed to float within a certain range rather than forced to take on a fixed number (the range is between 7.75 and 7.85 HKD to the USD). We believe that within five years the Yuan will become freely convertible in the world currency markets and, shortly after this happens, we believe that the HK dollar will detach itself from the US dollar and peg itself to the Yuan. At this time, we expect to see the Hong Kong dollar appreciate against other major currencies, such as the US dollar and the British pound.

Our big investment idea is to customize your own BRIC investment product, selecting a heavier weighting for China – we recommend a weighting of around 50 per cent, with the other three countries sharing the other 50 per cent. Unless you have a particular favourite in the remaining three countries, we suggest you invest 16.67 per cent of your BRIC in Brazil, 16.67 per cent in Russia and 16.67 per cent in India.

Now to the practical side of things: how do you go about actually buying into BRICs or building your own BRIC? There are a number of products available that are pre-packaged as a BRIC, but the disadvantage of this approach is that you are at the mercy of the fund manager to select the weightings across the four countries. For example, State Street Global Advisors has an exchange-traded fund (ETF) called The SPDR S&P BRIC 40 ETF (symbol BIK), which is weighted approximately as: Brazil (25.5 per cent), Russia (19 per cent), India (6.27 per cent) and China (49.22 per cent). (This information was updated in January 2009, so please check the State Street website for the latest percentages: www.spdrs.com)

There is also an ETF called the Claymore ETF (symbol EEB), which is weighted approximately as: Brazil (48 per cent), Russia (3 per cent), India (10 per cent) and China (39 per cent).

There is a third BRIC ETF to consider, managed by iShares (part of Barclays). It is called iShares MSCI BRIC Index Fund (symbol BKF), which has a different allocation again: Brazil (30 per cent), India (15 per cent), Russia (13.5 per cent), China (35 per cent) and Hong Kong (6.5 per cent).

The State Street and iShares ETFs have a closer weighting to our recommendation than the Claymore ETF, i.e. 50 per cent China, so these would be more closely aligned with our advice.

These BRICs are all listed in the US and denominated in US dollars.

Those of you who have the time and inclination to build your own BRIC can use the following listed products, which essentially track the stock market index of each country. This list of ETFs is by no means exhaustive but will give you a good feel of the BRIC country ETFs currently available:

- For Brazil, there is the iShares MSCI Brazil Index ETF, which trades under the symbol EWZ.
- For Russia, there is the Market Vector Russia ETF Trust, which trades under the symbol RSX.
- For India, there is the Barclays iPath MSCI India exchange traded note, which trades under the symbol INP. There is also the WisdomTree India Earnings Fund (ETF), which trades under the symbol EPI.
- For China, there is the PowerShares Golden Dragon Halter USX China ETF, which trades under the symbol PGJ.

Finally, for those of you interested in the long-term outlook for Vietnam, we recommend that you participate through investing in a managed fund specializing in Vietnam equities. There is also another risk that investors in Vietnam are particularly exposed to: because its stock market is relatively small in terms of the combined market capitalization of the companies listed on it, it can be rather volatile. It is not a market for the faint-hearted.

One fund that focuses on Vietnam that you might consider is the JF Vietnam Opportunities Fund. JP Morgan launched this fund in November 2006. It is an open-ended fund (the meaning of this is explained in Chapter Four, which covers funds) and invests in listed securities in Vietnam or companies that are listed elsewhere but have major operations in Vietnam. It trades under the Bloomberg ticker of JFVNOPP:KY. But be warned, there is a hefty 5 per cent front end fee to invest into this fund, so you may be better off looking to see if any new, recently-launched funds have lower fees. There is also a Vietnam-based asset manager called Dragon Capital (www.dragoncapital.com) which has a range of Vietnam funds; the largest of these is Vietnam Enterprise Investments Limited which was launched back in 1995. But this fund requires a minimum investment of US$100,000 so may not be suitable to most readers.

To access free quotes and charts for stocks, funds and ETFs, we recommend using Bloomberg, Yahoo Finance or Google Finance.

BigIdea # 8

At this point, we would also like to introduce another *BigIdea* that came to us when assessing the significance of mankind's enlarged footprint as a result of the fast developing BRIC economies. Our next *BigIdea* is **water**.

Without water, no forms of life can exist on earth. Water is absolutely vital to all of us and if each of us doesn't get to drink at least a litre of it every day, we would eventually die.

Furthermore, water is vital for plant and food growth, for industrial processes of every type, for washing and cooling, and for so much else that, in many ways, we all take for granted.

Dirty or polluted water is the biggest killer on earth, accounting for more deaths than malaria and AIDS put together. Four children every minute die of water-related disease in the third world.

Although the world has plenty of water and the total amount has remained constant for at least a million years, the distribution, cleanliness and availability of water pose major problems in many parts of the world.

It is estimated that at least one billion people – or one in six of us – drinks only polluted or dirty water on a daily basis. And that half of the world's population has no access to clean water for washing and other daily functions.

Climate change is accelerating the 'drying' of large parts of the world, as is the relatively inefficient use of water in agriculture since the 'green' revolution started in the 1960s.

In Australia, drought has become a regular feature of the country's summers, with devastating effects on agriculture. Even London's long-term rainfall has now fallen below that of Nairobi – all due to climate change.

It is estimated, for instance, that the world's food supply has more than doubled since the 'green revolution' in agronomics began, but that the consumption of water to produce that food has trebled. New forms of seeds and cultivation have exponentially expanded the use of water in crop production.

This has had the effect of draining aquifers and lowering the water tables in many developing countries, sometimes at an alarming rate. In India, for instance, the water table is at an all-time low. In some parts of India, the water table has fallen to 300 feet from 20 feet – and all in the space of ten years.

Two-thirds of the world's water that is taken from the environment is used to irrigate crops or to grow food. It takes 2000–5000 litres of water to produce just one kilogram of rice. Similarly, it takes over 11,000 litres of water to produce the feedstock for just one quarter-pound hamburger equivalent.

Countries such as India and Pakistan, where 400 cubic kilometres of water are drawn out of the water table every year to irrigate crops, are dangerously depleting their supplies of water.

Other countries, such as Sri Lanka, Indonesia, Iran and Bangladesh – not forgetting China, which is suffering from perennial droughts – share the same issues.

Almost every industrial process uses massive quantities of water also. One small car uses 450,000 litres in its production and even a T-shirt requires about 1000 litres.

This has led to the description of 'virtual' water as a means of describing the way in which water gets shipped around the world 'virtually' in the form of traded goods. This global trade in water is estimated at 20 Nile River equivalents per annum. One tonne of wheat exported from the United States requires 100 tonnes of 'virtual' water to produce it. The Middle East is so short of water that it imports 80–90 per cent of its water in the form of food.

Put another way, the gross excess of water consumption, for each one of of us who live in the West, amounts to about 100 times our own body weight.

And yet, half the world's population has no access to reasonable and clean water supplies.

No wonder there has been talk of 'water wars', and disputes over water rights are mounting, both between nations and between different parts of individual countries.

It strikes us that one of the reasons why water is used so inefficiently is because it is too cheap. We have got used to water being priced cheaply in almost the entire developed world.

That will change, over time, and with it emerges our *BigIdea* – profiting from the developing industries that seek to make water cleaner, safer, and more accessible. This industry is a relatively difficult one for us to invest in because it tends to be dominated by very large conglomerates – like Siemens of Germany or General Electric of the United States, where the water-related components of their businesses are rather small.

Alternatively, there are plenty of private companies in the industry, but sadly these are not accessible to us as investors.

But there are SOME opportunities for us to look at.

The key areas in water technology for us to research are:

1 **Desalination** – where salt water from the sea is converted into either potable (that is, drinking) or usable (i.e. for all other purposes) water.
2 **Water treatment plants and technology** – i.e. cleaning and recycling water.
3 **Water leak prevention technology** – pipes around the world are responsible for enormous waste in the eventual delivery of water to the end user.
4 **Increased efficiencies in the use of water** – it has been estimated, for instance, that the world could produce as much food as it currently does with just ONE THIRD of its current water consumption.

The global water industry has been estimated at over US$300 billion by the UK Trade and Industry Department, so the scale of the opportunity is vast.

Investors should look at the website of the Water Research Foundation, www.waterresearchfoundation.org, for a good deal of useful information on what is happening in the world of water technology.

Similarly, www.wateronline.com offers a very good compendium of developments in the industry.

In terms of stocks, we would recommend looking at the following:

1 **The PowerShares Water Resources Portfolio ETF**, traded in the US (symbol: PHO) – well diversified portfolio of water-related shares.

2 **Doosan Heavy Industries and Construction**, a South Korean company – the largest company involved in building desalination plants in the world. Trades in South Korea and the US (symbol: 034020).

3 **Halma** (symbol: HLMA), listed on the London Stock Exchange – a world leader in leak detection. This company has excellent management and a good long-term track record.

4 **Veolia Environnement** of France – the world's leader in terms of water treatment and recycling plants. This stock trades actively in New York (symbol: VE).

5 **Pico Holdings, US listed** (symbol: PICO), which has bought up considerable 'water rights' in Arizona and Nevada .

Chapter*Seven*

Commodities and Collectables

Commodities

There is no doubt that you will have seen at least one article about commodities in a newspaper or watched a programme about them on the television within the past year. Over the past few years, commodities have certainly been under the spotlight and have gone from lacklustre performer to the talk of the investment town. After reaching record highs in the first half of 2008, commodity prices then experienced record percentage falls in the second half of the year. So it has certainly been turbulent times for commodities. Was there a bubble that burst? Did forced sellers, hedge funds and specula tors amplify the upward and downward price movements? What are commodity prices likely to do over the next ten years?

Before we answer these questions and discuss whether there are still investment opportunities in commodities, let's go back to basics first and explain what commodities actually are and how they play their part in the investment markets and, indeed, global trade.

A commodity is a fungible good, or one that is interchangeable with other commodities of the same type. For example, if we wanted to buy a gallon of pure, distilled water (a commodity), it would not matter where or who we bought it from as it would be the same product. The only thing that would matter is the price, which constantly changes based on many factors that ultimately impact or are perceived to impact supply or demand of that product.

There are some 20 exchanges around the world where commodities can be traded; the most well-known ones are in Chicago and London. All sorts of commodities can be traded. They can be metals such as gold, platinum and titanium, or oil, or agricultural (soft) commodities such as soy, wheat, cocoa, coffee and sugar. These exchanges, however, do not trade the physical commodities on site – imagine the chaos of trading millions of tonnes of commodities across the trading floor every day. Instead, a buyer will negotiate with a seller and secure a contract agreeing to buy a specific amount of a commodity on a certain date at a specified price. The buyer typically only needs to put down a 5 per cent deposit to secure the deal. The investment is therefore very leveraged or geared.

Commodity exchanges are used by buyers who sincerely wish to acquire actual commodities; for example, a manufacturer of coaxial cables needs to ensure that it has sufficient copper for its production to meet customer orders. However, the vast majority of contracts are traded without taking possession of the underlying commodity, i.e. people buy or sell (short) a particular commodity, expecting its price to go up or down before the contract settlement date, and then buy or sell it back to another buyer through the exchange, hopefully at a profit.

For example, if coffee was trading at $1 per pound and Mr Bean bought $10,000 of it (10,000 pounds) through a 'futures' contract, i.e. a forward dated contract, he would only have to put down $500 to secure the contract and the balance on the settlement date. If Mr Bean ran a large chain of coffee shops, he would wait until the settlement date and then pay the balance to the seller before taking possession of the coffee, whereupon he would ship it to his warehouse for distribution to his coffee shops. If Mr Bean were a trader, however, he would have no intention of actually buying $10,000 worth of coffee so he would have purchased the contract purely because he believed that between the purchase date and the contract settlement date, the price of coffee would have risen. So if, say one week before the settlement date, the market price for coffee is $1.10, then Mr Bean could sell the coffee for $11,000 and make $1000 profit. Considering Mr Bean only put down $500, that's a 100 per cent return on his investment. But as we all know, prices can go down as well as up, and if the price of coffee dropped to $0.90, Mr Bean would have to sell his coffee for $9000 and walk away with $1000 loss. Of course, he could always take ownership of the coffee and hope the market turns again, but then there are logistical costs of moving and storing the coffee to consider as well as its shelf-life.

Another thing worth mentioning briefly is that commodity futures contracts can be used as a hedge. Let's use another example to illustrate this. Suppose that our Mr Bean is back to owning that chain of coffee shops and he wants to make sure that in six months' time his company is not driven out of business in the event that coffee prices increase substantially, eroding the profit margin from his business. To hedge against this eventuality, he could take out a futures contract entitling him to buy an agreed amount of coffee at a fixed price in six months' time. That will allow Mr Bean to know with certainty the cost of his primary raw material for a period of time, thus mitigating what he may consider to be the greatest risk to his business and allowing him to set the retail price of his coffee knowing that there is a sufficient profit margin included.

So in basic terms, that's what commodities are, how they are traded, why they are traded and the type of people who buy and sell them. Fundamental to all commodities is the simple balance of supply and demand. This dictates the price of all commodities – too much supply and the price goes down, a shortage and the price goes up.

This brings us nicely to the reason why we believe commodities offer an incredible investment opportunity over the next ten years. If the global supply of a commodity is growing at an annual rate of, say, 5 per cent (through the discovery of new mines, increased production of existing mines or through increased recycling), and the global demand for this same commodity is increasing at an annual rate of, say, 15 per cent, then it stands to reason that as long as demand growth is outstripping supply growth, the price of that commodity will rise and continue to rise until such time that a new supply–demand balance is reached.

Let's use an example with oil. Global oil demand is expected to rise by over 50 per cent in the first quarter of the 21st century. Much of this increased demand is and will continue to come from Asia, particularly China and India who are increasingly hungry for the stuff as their economies grow and industrialize further. Unfortunately, the global production levels of oil, i.e. the supply (not reserves) are forecast to increase only slightly. It stands to reason, therefore, that the price of oil will continue to rise for at least the next decade until technological breakthroughs are made that provide an alternative energy source, which would allow demand for oil to fall.

Despite the large falls in commodity prices in the second half of 2008, commodity prices are still up by over 160 per cent since 2000 according to the Commodity Price Index published in *The Economist* newspaper every week. We believe that they are still at the beginning of a long upward cycle that will continue to drive prices higher for much of the next decade. The price falls of commodities in 2008 make them even more attractive as a long-term investment.

The ongoing industrialization of the BRIC economies (Brazil, Russia, India and China) that we discussed in Chapter Six will create unprecedented demand for certain commodities and, given the limited availability of many of these commodities, prices will continue to rise. We also believe that the same applies to soft commodities (i.e. those commodities that tend to be grown rather than mined, such as cotton, wheat and cocoa, versus copper, gold, silver and platinum). These BRIC economies will certainly undergo an economic slowdown as a result of the global financial crisis, but eventually there will be a recovery, and the BRICs, especially China and India, will be at the forefront of that recovery.

So yes, we're big fans of investing in commodities even though there has been a great deal of media coverage on them over the past few years. Here are five reasons why:

Reason 1

It's an inflationary hedge. Inflation has become so widespread (although it is not accurately reported by official statistics) that it has eaten away at the purchasing power of our hard-earned money. Notice how little a dollar or a pound can buy you today, compared to, say, ten years ago? You can thank inflation for that. Commodity prices will hold up against inflation as they are linked to real, physical assets that have a limited supply, unlike cash – central banks can print as much cash as they need to fund governments' shopping lists and to cover any shortfalls in tax revenue.

Reason 2

Demand for commodities will continue to increase. As we mentioned earlier, the economic awakening of the BRIC economies, particularly China and India, which are home to almost 60 per cent of the world's population, will continue to drive demand for commodities. China has almost no commodities of its own and must rely on imports to allow it to develop its country's infrastructure and economy. For example, China is already the world's largest importer of steel and the second largest importer of oil, after the United States (and they might have reached the number one spot by the time you read this book).

Reason 3

It's an investment hedge/diversification strategy. Barring a systemic collapse of the financial system, there is no correlation between the price of commodities and other investments, such as equities, bonds and real estate so if these other asset classes came under pressure, you will at least have part of your investment in something that will not be affected.

Reason 4

Twenty-five per cent of global trade is in commodities so they have been around for a while and will continue to be the backbone of the global economy.

Reason 5

It's a new investment class that most retail investors like us have not had access to until recently. There are now effective ways to access what has traditionally been an asset class that has had substantial barriers to entry.

In order to really illustrate the incredible returns that some commodities have had, we have written a case study for one particular commodity that has had a truly remarkable return on investment since 2005 – uranium. Although we are not using uranium as one of our *BigIdeas*, it is still showing some further upside for those who are tempted.

Case Study: Uranium

Uranium is a somewhat controversial element – it can be used for good or evil, i.e. to generate efficient, clean and cheap energy, or to make nuclear weapons. As an aside, this is what the political stand-off between Iran and the rest of the world is all about – Iran claims it is seeking to generate energy from nuclear power, while the rest of the world believes it is just an excuse to produce nuclear weapons, especially given the fact that Iran is home to the world's third largest proven oil reserves so it doesn't really need an alternative source of energy.

Uranium is an incredibly efficient way of generating clean energy. To date, nuclear power generates 16 per cent of the world's energy supply and we believe this will increase substantially in the coming decade. Some countries are bigger fans of nuclear energy than others. France, for example, is a big proponent of nuclear energy and has 59 nuclear power stations that generate around 80 per cent of its energy. To do this, France needs around 10,000 tonnes of uranium every year

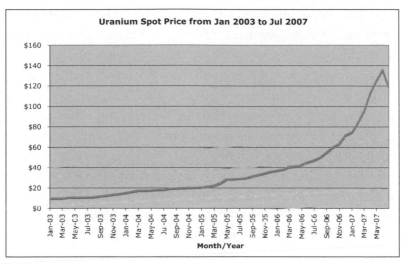

Uranium Spot Price from Jan 2003 to Jul 2007

Source: The Ux Consulting Company LLC.

which it acquires from the lucky few countries who have uranium deposits, namely Canada, Australia, Niger, Russia, Namibia, Kazakhstan and Russia. It may surprise some readers but in terms of the total power generated, the United States is actually the world's largest producer of nuclear-generated electricity, France is second followed by Japan. According to the IAEA (the International Atomic Energy Agency), there were 438 nuclear power stations in the world by the end of 2008 and another 44 under construction.

Current global annual uranium production is around 50,000 tonnes per year, which barely meets 60 per cent of the demand. The balance remaining has been obtained through the recycling of spent fuel rods, depleting stockpiles and by using up the weapons-grade uranium left over from the cold war. These alternative sources are running out.

Pound for pound, uranium generates almost two and a half MILLION times more energy than coal – and with no carbon dioxide emissions. There really isn't anything else that can even come close to rivalling uranium as an efficient and clean energy source. We know that some of you are thinking that nuclear power is an extremely dangerous source of energy with radioactive waste that lasts tens of thousands of years. Granted, nuclear energy tends to have negative connotations but that is primarily due to the word 'nuclear', which is immediately associated with death and destruction because of the nuclear bomb, but nuclear power is an entirely different application. There was also the infamous Chernobyl nuclear power plant accident in 1986, but that power station had a flawed design and an ineffective emergency shutdown procedure.

Today's nuclear power stations have technologies and processes in place that would render a repeat of that incident an extremely unlikely event. It is true that nuclear waste in the form of plutonium is an undesirable by-product of nuclear power and its disposal is a serious concern. Because it is highly radio-active and has a half-life of around 25,000 years (it takes this long for its radiation levels to fall by 50 per cent), the common way to dispose of it is to secure it in a container that prevents any of the radiation from leaking and to bury it deep in the ground or the ocean. Admittedly this is not ideal, but the amount of 'waste' produced for the power generated is very low. Perhaps there will be a breakthrough in the near future that would drastically reduce the radiation levels of nuclear waste through some chemical treatment – this would only strengthen the case for nuclear power further.

The world's biggest producers of uranium are Canada, Australia and Kazakhstan. These three countries alone accounted for 60 per cent of the uranium that was mined in the world in 2007.

BigIdea # 9

So on with our our next *BigIdea*, which you may have figured out by now is commodities. It all comes down to the basics of supply and demand. Despite the recent market turmoil, we still believe that the long-term demand for commodities will continue to steadily increase, wheras the supply side won't, so the price will go up. In fact, the 2008 tumble in commodity prices has resulted in even less supply as companies have closed down mines that are no longer profitable and put new mining projects on hold. The same goes for many of the soft commodities. But when does supply start to increase to bring prices back down? Not for many more years. Commodity prices usually cycle in 20–30 year intervals, the reason being that there is a long lead time involved in sourcing new supply to the market. Because most commodities are only recently coming out of rock-bottom prices, there has been no incentive for the industry to invest in new technologies or to source new supplies – until now. But we are only six years, at best, into the next cycle, so we won't be seeing new supply overnight. Eventually, by the end of the cycle, we can expect to see prices come back down. One can't just open a new mine and start production overnight – these things take years from the time prospecting starts to when supply actually hits the market.

Developed and emerging economies alike will continue to buy more commodities to build their lacking infrastructure, but the main piston of growth will still be China. As we mentioned earlier, China is already the world's largest consumer of steel and the second-largest consumer of oil. But China is only just beginning to modernize its vast and populous nation. There are many more cities that are only just starting to develop (see the section on China in Chapter Six), so the massive demand for raw materials to feed this growth isn't going to abate. Again, we are taking the long-term, ten-year view – even the gloomiest forecasters expect the global economy to recover well before then.

There are other emerging economies with growing appetites for raw materials, albeit less ravenous than China's. Until the middle of 2008, much of East Asia experienced its best growth since the Asia Financial Crisis in 1997/98, which brought the economies of these countries to their knees.

But with so many commodities to choose from, which ones are likely to perform the best over the next ten years? Our belief is that extractive metals will be best performers. Our reasoning is that the further industrialization of commodity-poor China and, to a lesser extent, the other emerging markets of India, South America and South East Asia, will continue to drive demand for these metals for the next decade, while at the same time their supply will remain very limited.

More specifically, the extractive metals we are recommending are copper and zinc.

Copper

As you can see from the chart, the price of copper has had a phenomenal run over the past five years or so. Like other commodities, its price tumbled as the global markets went into chaos during the last quarter of 2008. Investors across the board either panicked and sold or were forced to sell and close their positions due to margin calls on their leveraged holdings. Demand also slowed due to the general slowing down in the global economy. The result was a violent fall in the price of copper. Even so, our long-term view for copper remains very positive.

Unlike certain other commodities, copper is not rare so it is not purchased for a store of value in the same way that gold or platinum are. In fact, quite the opposite: according to the Copper Development Association (a US-based body), global copper resources are estimated to be almost 5.8 trillion pounds (that's around 2.6 trillion kilograms for our metric readers) and about 12 per cent of it has already been mined.

So if there's so much copper on this planet, why did its price set record highs in the first half of 2008? The reason is that it isn't being mined quickly enough to meet the growing global demand and new supply will not be coming online any time soon – there hasn't been a new major copper mine discovery for around 100 years. Once the

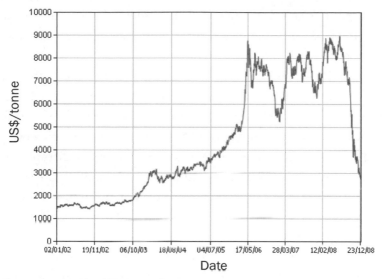

Source: London Metal Exchange. Reproduced by permission of www.lme.com

global economy recovers, the demand trend for copper will resume, as will its upward price movement.

Copper is used to make so many things – it's the third most widely-used metal. Examples of its uses include electrical and electronic products, transportation equipment and consumer and general products. It is the backbone of telecommunications, where endless miles (or kilometres) help us to stay in touch and network together. The total length of copper wires used in telecommunications alone would circle the globe many times over. Copper is also found in every home – it is used for wiring and plumbing. Now think of all the new homes and buildings that are going up in all the emerging economies around the world, especially China, which has over 100 cities with over one million people. Think of all the electrical grid systems being built in those cities and countries. Demand will only grow stronger and there appears to be no substitute for copper's combination of malleability, ductile strength, resistance to corrosion, and electrical conductivity (second only to silver). And, by the way, brass is made from copper and zinc and it too has many uses, especially as a decorative trim in residential and commercial applications. A few examples include door hinges, hand-rails and door knobs.

Although there are quite a few countries that produce copper, by far the world's largest producer is Chile (much of it through the state-owned firm Codelco), accounting for over a third of global production. Chile is to copper what Saudi Arabia is to oil. However, Chile's copper production is down as a result of a few disruptions – striking miners and a severe earthquake in June 2005 (measuring 7.8 on the Richter scale) to name a couple of the serious ones. Other copper-producing countries include the US, Canada, Russia, Peru and Australia.

So how can you go about investing in copper? Of course, we don't recommend that you go out and buy copper futures, even if you did know how to do that. Our recommendation is to invest in a fund specializing in metals/extractive metals or to invest in a large, stable mining company – an American, Canadian or Australian one, or even a South African one for the braver investors.

There is now an ETF dedicated to tracking the price of copper. It is listed on the London Stock Exchange under the symbol COPA and is valued in US dollars. However, at the time of writing, the size of the fund was only $11 million, so please consider this when using this ETF as your exposure to copper.

A second ETF to consider is one that tracks a broader basket of metals and mining companies. It is managed by State Street and trades on the New York Stock Exchange under the name of SPDR S&P Metals and Mining ETF (symbol XME). At the time of researching, this fund comprised a holding of 24 companies ranging from Freeport-McMoRan Copper & Gold Inc. (the world's largest publicly-traded copper company) to Arch Coal Inc. (America's largest coal producer). So it's a 'blue chip' diversified commodity fund with exposure to copper but also other commodities. More information about XME and its manager State Street can be found at www.spdrs.com/product/fund.seam?ticker=XME.

A third option is to invest directly in a mining company, such as Southern Copper Corporation. This company is listed on the New York Stock Exchange under the symbol PCU. It has a market capitalization of $13 billion (in January 2009) and a PE (price to earnings) ratio of 7. All of its mines and production facilities are located in Mexico and Peru. It is also a producer of molybdenum, zinc and silver. Based on the closing stock price at the end of 2008, PCU paid out a healthy dividend yield of 12 per cent for that year. Its website can be found at: www.southernperu.com.

Zinc

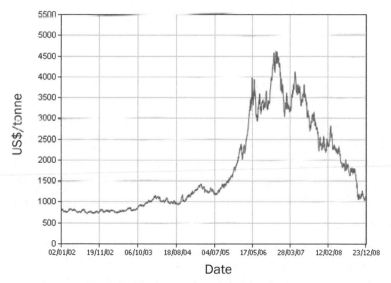

Source: London Metal Exchange. Reproduced by permission of www.lme.com

Zinc is another extractive metal we believe will become more expensive as a result of the continued development of the emerging countries, particularly the BRIC economies. As you can see from the chart, like copper, it too had a good run over the past few years; then fell sharply in the second half of 2008, as did virtually all commodities. Zinc is the other element used in making brass, but what are its other applications?

The largest and most important application of zinc is in the galvanization of iron and steel. As we all know, iron and steel have many uses, but their biggest weakness is that they tend to rust when exposed to the atmosphere for prolonged periods of time. That is because the iron (steel is primarily made of iron with a small percentage of carbon) reacts with the oxygen in the air. Rust causes corrosion which then compromises the physical properties of the iron and steel. This is where zinc comes to the rescue – a thin layer of zinc is used to coat the exposed iron or steel and thus protect it from rust. Without forcing you to revisit your school chemistry classes, suffice to say that zinc more readily reacts with oxygen than iron does and it 'sacrifices' itself to keep the iron oxide free. The zinc coating does wear off but the rate depends on the thickness of the coating and the harshness of the environment.

Zinc is also used as the anode (the positive end) of batteries as well as for making die castings which are used in manufacturing, such as the automobile industry.

After iron, aluminium (or aluminum for our North American readers) and copper, zinc is usually the fourth most widely-used metal.

If you can't find an extractive metals commodity fund that you are happy with, you can consider investing in zinc directly. By this we don't mean that you should buy zinc futures, but rather we recommend that you buy an ETF that tracks the price of zinc. One such ETF trades under the symbol ZINC on the London Stock Exchange. But in the wake of the market turmoil in 2008, the market capitalization of this fund has fallen to just $8 million. Please factor this into your investment decision.

There is also a listed company in Canada called Canadian Zinc Corporation (trading under the symbol CZN) that you can consider looking into. The company's website is www.canadianzinc.com.

Another company to consider is an Australian listed firm by the name of Kagara Zinc Limited, trading under the symbol KZL (website: www.kagara.com.au).

The stock prices of these and all mining companies have suffered during the big commodity sell-off of the second half of 2008. However, we maintain that in our ten-year time horizon, copper and zinc are still excellent long-term investments whose prices will be the first to rally at the first signs of an economic recovery.

Platinum

Although not directly under this *BigIdea*, we thought we'd mention platinum purely because of its rarity. Platinum is the rarest of all precious metals – about 30 times rarer than gold. If you were able to pour the world's supply of platinum into a 50-metre Olympic size swimming pool, it would barely cover your ankles. The global annual supply of platinum is between 100 to 130 tonnes. Almost the entire world's supply of platinum is located in four countries: South Africa (with almost 80 per cent of the world's supply), Russia, Canada and the US. There are no reserves of platinum anywhere in the world so supply cannot be manipulated as it can with diamonds.

Annual platinum consumption is divided into three categories: 50 per cent industrial uses; 40 per cent jewellery manufacturing; and 10 per cent for investment purposes.

Platinum may already make up a component of some diversified commodity funds, but if it isn't and you would like to invest in platinum directly, then consider the following companies:

- **Anglo Platinum** – symbol AMS, listed on the South African Stock Exchange, although it has operations and explorations worldwide, including risky but perhaps eventually rewarding Zimbabwe (website: www.angloplatinum.com).
- **Aquarius Platinum** – this company is listed on three stock exchanges – Australia, London and South Africa – all under the symbol AQP. It has operations primarily in South Africa but also in risky Zimbabwe. In addition to platinum, the company mines palladium, rhodium, ruthenium, iridium and osmium (website: www.aquariusplatinum.com).

These are just a couple of investment ideas for those looking at investing in platinum.

Gold

Whilst we don't consider gold as being one of our *BigIdeas* either, we will briefly discuss it as it can be a sensible and stable part to any investment portfolio.

Gold is a long-recognized global currency that has a finite supply. It is traditionally a safe haven in times of uncertainty and many of us living in the Anglo-Saxon economies are confronted with a delicate economic balancing act: on the one hand, we are faced with inflationary pressures as a result of central banks keeping lending rates artificially low for most of this century to stimulate spending; and on the other we have a globally integrated financial system that is severely indebted and vulnerable to rising interest rates (because the repayment amounts on loans increase, as any mortgage holder will attest).

At the first sign of trouble, gold is the safe haven of choice and stands to benefit from economic uncertainty.

There are many companies to choose from when seeking to buy into gold-related investments. Investing directly in one gold mining company is rather riskier than buying gold directly; unless you have time to monitor the company or companies you are investing in, you risk losing a lot of money because mining companies are a high-risk investment – the mine they have spent the past six months working on may be a dud or may contain a fraction of the resources they believed it to have initially. For this reason, we suggest that readers invest in a basket of mining companies to remove the risk of a single point of failure.

The following three are suggested funds or trusts that track the price of gold:

- **Central Fund of Canada Limited** (symbol: CEF) – a specialized, self-governing, passive holding company with most of its assets held in **gold** and **silver** bullion. At 13 January, 2009, 96.8 per cent of Central Fund's net assets consisted of unencumbered, segregated, insured, passive holdings of gold and silver bullion, the rest being held in cash. Central Fund is required to maintain a minimum of 90 per cent of its net assets in gold and silver bullion, of which at least 85 per cent must be in physical form.

- **iShares COMEX Gold Trust** (symbol: IAU) – a grantor trust that seeks to correspond generally to the day-to-day movement of the price of gold bullion. The purpose of the trust is to own gold transferred to the trust in exchange for shares issued by the trust (iShares). Each iShare represents a fractional undivided beneficial interest in the net assets of the trust. The assets of the trust consist primarily of gold held by the custodian on behalf of the trust.

- **SPDR Gold Trust** (symbol: GLD) – is also an investment trust. The investment objective of the trust is for the shares to reflect the performance of the price of gold bullion. The shares are intended to offer investors an opportunity to participate in the gold market through an investment in securities.

Collectables

Collectables are an interesting asset class and are certainly not for everyone. They are usually items that are unique, in limited supply or fashionable, and tend to be objects of art or aesthetic beauty. Some people buy collectables to display and admire at home, while others buy them as investments with a view to selling them and making a financial gain at some point in the future. This is a book about creating and building wealth so it is only be the latter that are of interest to us.

A surge in activity in collectables is typically an indication of the last peak in an economic cycle and, given the recent press about the record prices 'art lovers' are paying for collectables, it would lead us to believe that we are indeed at the peak of an economic cycle. In 2006, a painting by Jackson Pollock sold for over US$140 million. Another two paintings, one by Willem de Kooning and the other by Gustav Klimt, also sold for around $140 million in that same year. The previous record for the most expensive painting was set back in 1990 for a Van Gogh. To us, these are not investments – they actually tie up cash that could be invested more wisely. After all, how long would you have to stare at one of these paintings before you felt that you had got your $140 million worth? Several lifetimes, we suspect.

Obviously we don't expect you to have $140 million of spare cash lying around that you were planning to sink into art because, if you did, you probably wouldn't be reading a book about wealth creation in the first place. The above does illustrate, though, how seemingly arbitrary the prices of collectables are and for this reason we think they are too unpredictable and volatile for the retail investor.

However, if you have a passion for a certain type of collectable, we certainly don't want to hold you back – but please read our cautionary advice before you take any further action. An investor in collectables must really do their homework before parting with the cash – unlike other investments, the value of collectables is extremely subjective and the channels for buying and selling them are more limited, as is their volume. In other words, they are illiquid. This may be problematic if you happen to own a certain type of collectable that suddenly falls out of favour as you would have trouble off-loading it in same way that you can easily sell a stock or a bond.

Conversely, if you've invested wisely, your investment could appreciate rather quickly if it became very fashionable. You would then have the fortune of auctioning it off to the highest bidder. It is important to stress the subjectivity of the value of collectables as they are typically worth far more than their underlying value; for example, a 'priceless' Picasso painting is simply made up of paint and canvas. The perceived value of such a painting is purely based on how much of a premium a buyer is prepared to pay. This goes for all collectables such as antiques, stamps, wine, art, jewellery, comic books, baseball cards, Persian carpets and vintage cars.

So unless you have a genuine interest in collectables and consider it as a hobby of sorts, then we recommend that you avoid them in your overall investment strategy – it's simply too easy to buy the wrong item, pay the wrong price and fall prey to scams.

If you're still reading this section, we are assuming that you do have a passion for collectables and would like to find out how you can turn that passion into profit.

Firstly, let's recap the key points from this section to make sure you really know what you're getting into:

- Collectables are one of the riskiest types of investment.
- Collectables are illiquid – there are no guarantees that you'll ever be able to find a future buyer for your collectable at a higher price than you paid.
- Collectables are particularly vulnerable to economic down-turns.
- Prices for collectables are determined by factors such as rarity, condition, age and fads. It's what a buyer is prepared to pay for it that ultimately will determine the price.
- Don't buy any collectables until you've done your research. Read books, magazines, attend auctions, visit antique dealers, go to antique road shows and surf the Internet.
- Successful collectors are passionate about the items they collect. But don't get too emotionally attached to an item and pay too much for it .

As a ground rule, we recommend that you invest a maximum of 5 per cent of your portfolio in collectables, even if you know or think you know what you are doing.

We are not going to claim that we are experts in all collectables, but we have both invested in them with success. Two areas we are more comfortable with are art and wine.

If you're interested in investing in art work, you should attend a few auctions to get a feel for what it's all about. Auction houses are the most popular venue for selling art work, especially paintings, which make up about three-quarters of all the sales revenue of auction houses globally. If you're not sure where your nearest auction house is, visit www.artnet.com/auctionhousedirectory/index.asp for a comprehensive list. The main website, www.artnet.com, is an excellent source of information for those interested in investing in art from buying trends, upcoming auctions, prices, artists and galleries.

For wine, you can consider investing in a wine fund as well as physically purchasing a selection of wine that you believe will appreciate over time. Bordeaux is the most popular wine to invest in, largely because of its consistently high-quality vintages, very limited supply and high brand awareness. A couple of wine funds which are accessible to retail investors that are worth considering are The Wine Investment Fund and The Fine Wine Fund. These are typically five-year closed-end funds, meaning that you put your money in and you can't take it out until the end of the fund's life, at which point you will hopefully get more than your initial investment amount.

Empirical data does suggest that there is no correlation between the performance of stocks and bonds and that of fine wine. It could therefore be considered as a diversification strategy to an investment portfolio.

For more details about investing in fine wine, visit the websites of The Wine Investment Fund (www.wineinvestmentfund.com) and The Fine Wine Fund (www.thefinewinefund.com). The minimum investment amount for these funds is £10,000, so you need to determine whether this would make up more than 5 per cent of your portfolio as you should not be over-exposed to one specific asset class, particularly a risky one such as collectables.

Chapter*Eight*

Green Investments

We all know that the world is undergoing some fundamental environmental changes and at a rate unprecedented in recorded history. The question that this book is in part seeking to answer is: how can we, as investors, turn these changes and trends – some of which are staring us right in the face – into tangible monetary returns on investment?

With that in mind, anyone halfway serious about *BigIdea* investing will already be looking at the area that has gained a 'tipping point' of media attention of late: **climate change**.

Beyond the hype, and the mostly token gestures that individuals and governments alike are making, a genuine and potentially devastating crisis is emerging. It may not seem so as we write this in the midst of a cold winter, but it is happening. This crisis will eclipse the financial turmoil of 2008–09, which is, of course, reversible. Unlike the latter, the climate crisis will pose a threat to all future generations.

This crisis has already started to capture the attention of some of the brightest minds of the current scientific and business generation. This brainpower is busy figuring out new and innovative ways to address the predicament we face as a result of continued and accelerating industrialization: how to counter its clearly adverse environmental effects. Already, large-scale funding by venture capitalists and others is changing the face of Silicon Valley in California. Instead of being focused primarily on computer-related technology, the world's pre-eminent centre of innovation is reshaping itself as the centre for 'green' innovation.

Just to rehearse the obvious, there are two distinct problems. One relates to a growing population, limited fresh water supply, constrained supplies of raw materials and of commodities; the other is of course rising greenhouse gas emissions, the vast majority of which is carbon dioxide.

The breakneck speed of mass industrialization, beginning in the 1820s but accelerating in our own era as a result of globalization, has been largely fuelled by the burning of fossil fuels.

There is clear scientific evidence that the burning of such fuels on such a scale has caused 'anthropogenic' or man-induced greenhouse gas emissions, including carbon dioxide, methane and nitrogen dioxide. All of these together are likely to be the principal cause of a process of global climate change that has meant a rise in the surface temperature of the earth of $0.6°$ C in the 20th century. The worst of all of these in terms of impact is carbon dioxide, and it is in the limitation of the emissions of that gas globally that there lies considerable investment opportunity.

We are not seeking in this book to make any form of political statement, but we can make one definitive assertion: **climate change is here**. Only the most obdurate and self-interested of us can think or believe otherwise.

Whether or not the clear trend towards global warming that we are experiencing is **definitely** caused by man-induced factors is quite another point – but the evidence points clearly to that being the case.

Regardless, even if man-made factors are not largely or exclusively to blame for damaging increases in global temperatures, there is now sufficient political will and economic incentive for dramatic changes in the way that energy is produced and consumed.

Therein lies an enormous opportunity for every investor on this planet.

Quite possibly, the biggest theme of all, in investment terms, over the next ten years will be the broadly defined 'green' movement. New methods of generating power, enhanced extraction techniques for existing sources of power, conservation measures, and changing fiscal regimes in relation to the use of power will all create one of the biggest global businesses.

This movement will dwarf anything seen in the Internet bubble years and will create real fortunes. It will also be a feast for opportunists with its fair share of charlatans, rogues and promoters – whose broken promises will litter many an investment portfolio.

In this section, we will help you to sort the wheat from the chaff, the jewels from the chicanery – and guide you to profit. And we have one specific *BigIdea* for you to explore. It's ubiquitous, it's essential to life and it's free – it's the sun.

But first, some background.

Self-preservation – which many scientists now believe we are actively promoting when we attempt to control climate change – has always been a powerful motivating factor for mankind.

Soon, the days when the US government and others, blinkered by self-interest, could stick their heads in the sand and pretend that climate change didn't exist, or was exaggerated, or wasn't their fault, will be over. The new President, Barack Obama, has promised to change that. Indeed, a key part of his 2009 platform for restoring growth in America is to use government sponsored spending on green projects to kick start the economy. Green spending in the US is set to soar, creating massive opportunities for entrepreneurs and investors. President Obama has committed to creating five million American jobs by investing $150 billion in renewable energy. By doing so, he hopes to double the energy production from renewables in just three years.

Similarly, the UK's Conservative leader David Cameron, who in our opinion will win the next general election, has released his new policy document 'The Low Carbon Economy'. The document states that 'decarbonising Britain will help create hundreds of thousands of jobs, raise skills and improve Britain's competitiveness'.

Even China plans to spend $142 billion of its stimulus package on environmental measures.

This governmental momentum, sponsoring what is in fact a whole new industry, is bolstered by mounting and incontrovertible evidence that a changing weather pattern is with us for **certain**. We are now at the tipping point, where the effort to reverse the perceived effects of manmade emissions on our climate will become a global effort.

No one yet knows exactly just how that effort will be manifested, but we have a few useful pointers to guide us:

1 The Kyoto Protocol, to which every major nation bar the US and Australia is a signatory, is a multinational attempt to limit carbon emissions. When the US joins – as it will now that Barack Obama is president – the form of these limits may become more concrete and the markets more certain about just what is allowed and what is not. A global, major and sustained effort to reduce carbon emissions will soon be reality.

2 The price of oil and of other key fossil fuels – coal and natural gas – is over time, generally rising, reflecting increased demand, particularly from the BRIC economies, as well as emerging supply shortages. In the current economic downturn, the price of oil and gas, like that of almost all other commodities, has fallen but, over time, it is set to rise further. Economic incentive is a powerful thing – and this is leading to multiple opportunities:

a) New exploration for fossil sources

b) Improved economics for the extraction of oil and gas from difficult fields

c) A spur to the creation of alternative sources of fuel, including so-called renewables. Linked to this is the amazingly fast development of new technologies to create and to conserve energy.

3 We can already take note that significant amounts of capital in almost every part of the world are being deployed to take advantage of these trends; new plants are being built to manufacture photovoltaic cells, for instance, for solar power projects; hydrogen fuel cells are being developed at a rapid rate to a point near commercialization; and nuclear power stations are being planned or built in quantity.

In addition, wind 'farms' now dot many landscapes. Huge amounts are being spent on bringing gas out of inhospitable locations – as well as oil out of tar sands. Swathes of land in the US, Europe and in Latin America are being turned over to growing 'bio' crops, used as fossil fuel substitutes.

All of these pointers are just a foretaste of what is to come. The whole 'renewables and new energy' industry is on the cusp of a breathtaking advance.

It is not for us to judge whether or not we may all be burnt to cinders by the sun in 30 years or so unless these developments are successful – it is only, for the purposes of this book, enough for us to say that this is a **gold rush** at its very earliest stages. And it's a gold rush that every serious investor should consider as one of his or her *BigIdeas*.

In considering how to invest in this sector, we think it best to divide the 'green' space up into several areas of potential opportunity:

1 **'Traditional' renewables.** These include: solar power, hydro (e.g. tidal and wave power), wind power, and conservation. In each of these areas, there is considerable potential for profit. As the scale of each of these industries expands, the cost of energy generated or saved by them will come down and their market potential will grow, i.e. these are the kinds of businesses that we like.

2 **'Hi tech'-based low carbon emission power sources.** These include: nuclear power, now enjoying a significant revival; hydrogen fuels cells; and sophisticated waste-to-energy projects.

3 **Improved use and extraction of fossil-based fuels.** This sector includes: drilling in inhospitable locations for untapped sources of oil; 'clean' coal; oil from tar sands; and conservation of fossil fuels through improved engine technologies and through better use of insulation in homes and public places.

4 **'Bio' energy.** Growing crops that can be used to create alternatives to fossil fuels.

5 **Conservation of the environment**, partly to reabsorb carbon dioxide emissions, which is believed to be the major cause of global warming. This takes the form of 'saving' the rainforest, of planting trees to absorb carbon emissions, and of such technologies as 'carbon sequestration' which involves storing carbon emissions deep in the earth's surface.

6 **Fiscal, monetary and 'tariff' measures** to encourage consumption of greener energy, and to limit the consumption of fossil-based energies.

All of these factors are at work in creating what already is – and will continue to be for many years to come – an enormous business opportunity for all of us.

We could devote the whole of this book to this developing industry; it has more potential than any other in our opinion. But we are not doing so for two reasons:

1 Every investor needs to DIVERSIFY – which is why we are providing ten quite separate *BigIdeas*, of which only one is in the green space. This doesn't mean that investors should slavishly follow us in limiting their investments to one element of the green sector, just that they should be aware that having too many eggs in this highly attractive basket carries risks.

2 Sooner or later, we all have to FOCUS on the particular way in which we individually take advantage of any *BigIdea*. In the case of renewables, there are quite a few areas that look interesting. But, ultimately, there is only one that we personally will be making a big play for. That's because we don't have the time to research, monitor and explore the myriad of possibilities within this investment space. And besides, it's become pretty obvious to us in the course of writing this book what our *BigIdea* in green investing should be.

BigIdea # 10

Our particular favourite *BigIdea* is **solar power**. This is because the factors that will drive its growth as an industry are those that we look for in the very best business opportunities, that is: *lower prices = expanded demand = MoneyFountain*.

In our opinion, solar power will provide investors with multiple opportunities. Among those will be opportunities in **utility**-scale power generation using the sun's energy, opportunities in the **manufacture** and distribution of new ways of harnessing the sun's power, and opportunities in **extractive** industries, which mine the key components of solar panels.

Generally speaking, the solar module (or PV cell for the purposes of our research) represents about 40–50 per cent of the total installed cost of a solar system. A complete solar system includes more than just solar cells – it also includes all the other components required to create a functioning system – to feed energy into the grid or to allow stand-alone off grid applications.

Whereas the oil industry uses the price per barrel as its key unit of price measurement, the solar industry uses 'price per watt peak'. This P/WP has fallen from about US$27 P/WP to just over US$2.50 P/WP today – a reduction of 90 per cent in 25 years, and the pace of that reduction is accelerating. That is one of the key reasons why we are so excited about solar power.

In this chapter, we will give specific guidance on where we see this solar industry going – and we will also discuss, but not to the same degree of detail, opportunities in other parts of the 'green' sector.

The combination of planetary necessity, political impetus and accelerating technology will make this area just about the most exciting to be over the next decade.

This is the Big Daddy of the BigIdeas and one that every investor should pay close attention to.

It wasn't until the industrial revolution, beginning in the 1820s, that mankind turned to non-renewable, fossil fuels as the principal source of power. Up to that point, mankind's history had been one of harnessing the sun, the wind, water and firewood to create energy. With the industrial revolution, and in particular the wide-scale use of coal and subsequently of oil, the entire balance of fuel consumption changed, and today the world is powered largely (about three quarters) by natural gas, oil and coal.

All of these are, to varying degrees, 'dirty' fuels, in that they expand the volume of carbon emissions. And all of these are finite in supply, though with a great deal of debate as to just how long any one of them will last.

Today, there is recognition that the balance of probability is that man-made consumption of fossil fuels is the major contributor to carbon emission-induced changing climate patterns. These emissions will have highly adverse future consequences if unchecked, and so the wheel of history has turned full circle.

This is because 'traditional' forms of sustainable, non-polluting energy – including wind, water and solar power – are once again in vogue, albeit in significantly different forms.

These are now joined by new forms of environmentally friendly power output – including certain types of farmed bio-mass fuels, waste-to-energy projects, and hydrogen fuel cells.

All the forms of renewable energy put together thus far make for a puny total output relative to total world energy consumption. It is a fact that the world increased its consumption of all types of energy by about ten times in the 20th century; the pace of that increase is now accelerating, with the breakneck development of the BRIC economies.

The United Nations estimated that in 2002, the total energy consumption for every man, woman and child on the planet was about 6 litres of oil equivalent per day, or 10.8 billion tonnes of energy equivalent per annum for the world in total.

Of that, over 75 per cent was fossil fuel based; the balance was made up of the 'sustainable' or 'near sustainable' forms of energy consisting of nuclear power (about 5 per cent); hydro (about 6 per cent); other renewables, such as solar and wind power (2 per cent); and traditional biomass, predominantly dung, peat and firewood (about 10 per cent).

Of course, not all of this latter is 'clean' or carbon-neutral energy – biomass is not, for instance, unless replaced at an equivalent rate by carbon-absorbing forests or plants as the biomass fuel is burned.

Coal, which remains the most abundant fossil fuel, is largely concentrated in Australia, China, the US and South Africa. Coal is fundamentally the most polluting of the major fossil fuels, followed by oil and then by natural gas.

Energy consumption varies widely across the world: North Americans consume about six tonnes of oil equivalent in energy per year; Europeans and people in the former Soviet Union about half that, and the rest of the world one sixth of the American per capita figure, or one tonne per head.

It is that 'rest of the world' figure which is rising at the fastest pace, as the BRIC economies develop. In the US, Europe and the developed world, the per capita consumption of energy is actually static and has been for 30 years or more, as efficiencies and conservation have been introduced. But because of the growth in 'the rest of the world' figures, total consumption of energy is rising with population growth. And this growth is heading into the brick wall of finite supply. Fossil fuels, as everyone knows, are running out.

As to when this will happen is a fairly haphazard guess: BP estimated in 2003 that coal at current rates of consumption would last for about 200 years – but, of course, coal is the dirtiest and therefore the least environmentally desirable fuel. Oil and gas are reaching peak output sometime now, and thereafter oil will last for about 40 more years and gas for about 60 years, at declining rates of production, according to BP. In other words, we don't have long – and that is being reflected in steadily rising prices for fossil fuels of all types.

However, the double whammy of the diminishing supplies of fossil fuels and a clearly changing climatic backdrop to our life on earth are at long last impelling governments to take action, albeit hesitatingly. And it is in the wake of their as yet feeble actions that the private sector is sniffing out and taking advantage of profitable opportunities.

These opportunities, as already mentioned, are manifold. For instance, between the burning of the power source (in the case of fossil fuels) and the final so-called useful energy (heated water, for instance), there is substantial leakage. This is because of inefficiencies in the delivery system, which in the case of most electrical supply is known as the 'grid', as well as in losses in all sorts of ways thereafter. Insufficient insulation, inefficient engines, misdirected heat and light sources and so on are additional contributors to energy wastage.

But in most countries, the biggest loss of potential energy is in the form of 'waste' heat in power stations. For instance, it is estimated that about 60 per cent of the energy input into the UK's public-supply power stations (in the form of coal, gas, nuclear heat, oil, waste materials, hydro and wind) is WASTED. This waste takes the form of heat dumped into the sea or through giant cooling towers.

In addition, about 8 per cent of power is estimated to be 'lost' as it is transmitted through the grid system to consumers.

In the case of the UK, this waste from power stations has been estimated at more than the country's entire use of energy to heat buildings and water – about a third of total energy demand (DTI 2001).

So, clearly, one growth industry for the future will be that which seeks to DELIVER energy in a more efficient manner (e.g. efficient power stations, efficient engines) and to CONSERVE it when it is delivered (better insulation, as an example). We will look at some aspects of this in our investment review of this sector.

But, in our opinion, the biggest industry of all will be the so-called RENEWABLE industry.

This is going to be so big because it ticks all of the right boxes: it is eco-friendly, it marches with the zeitgeist of our times, and it is in its absolute infancy.

As an example of how as yet 'unformed' this industry is, total renewable energy use in the UK is estimated today at only about 1 per cent of total energy usage, and at 2.6 per cent of electricity output.

In most other developed countries it is similarly low, except in countries such as Canada, where there is abundance of hydro-electrical output, or Denmark, where wind power now accounts for over 20 per cent of electricity production.

In the UK, the government wants to see the figure of just under 3 per cent of total electrical output from renewable sources rise to 10 per cent by 2010 (a most unlikely achievement) and to 20 per cent by 2020.

While these are aggressive targets, they are ones that appear to be generally supported by the UK population. And that support for a move to 'green energy' is replicated in most other developed nations. This is good news, because it means the political backdrop for a brand-new industry – sustainable energy production on a large scale – is apparent right around the world.

So from wind farms to tidal and wave projects; from waste-to-heat projects to more extensive nuclear generation; with, of course, solar power coming up on the rails – the race is on to transform the electrical energy-generating landscape of the world.

Perhaps the most visible of these initiatives occurs in the form of wind power. All across Europe, wind farms are sprouting like mushrooms. An industry once derided as a novelty is now a multi-billion euro/dollar sector all on its own.

Wind power is relatively cheap as renewable energy goes, and in many developed countries there are significant subsidies available to encourage its use. In modern usage, wind power is derived from so-called wind turbines (a term used to differentiate them from windmills). Wind power has really caught on as the price and efficiency of turbines have improved, particularly since the mid-1990s, and it is estimated that the industry has been growing for the past decade at about 40 per cent annually.

Today, there are about 50,000 Megawatts of installed wind turbine capacity around the world, with Europe in particular a heavy user (and subsidizer).

Winds are created by the differential effects of solar radiation at various latitudes around the world and clear wind patterns exist as a result. The proximity of sea and mountains also has an effect on the prevailing nature of winds, and it is no accident that many wind farms are situated in coastal or mountainous regions.

Wind turbine technology – and particularly the technology of the aerofoil (or what we might think of as the blade or propeller) – has advanced considerably in recent years.

The output power of any wind turbine differs according to a multiplicity of factors – including wind speed, shape of the aerofoil, efficiency of the turbine, speed of rotation, the need to shut down the blades if wind speed is too high, and the number of blades. Wind turbines are angled to 'see' the prevailing wind, and certain types are designed to turn whichever way the wind is coming from.

Each wind turbine has a so-called speed-power curve, with typical optimal efficiency at a wind speed of about 15–25 miles per hour.

There are equations available to scientists to determine the likely output of any given wind turbine on a specific site, but these rely on estimates of available wind over an annual period.

The wind power industry, while still in its relative infancy, is possibly the most sophisticated of all the renewables sectors. Complex wind speed maps and atlases have been developed; wind flow simulation computer models are widely available; wind turbine technology has become increasingly sophisticated, from the blades, to the gearboxes, to the reduction in transmission losses. There have been numerous studies about the environmental impact of wind farms. These range from noise, to electromagnetic interference, to the most obvious one of visual blight. These studies have helped to reduce the disruptive and unpleasant impact of early wind farms, but there is no getting away from the fact that wind farms occupy space, they are relatively unsightly, and they are dependent on windy days to generate electricity – as well as heavy subsidies in most countries.

There is a finite limit to what can be done by wind; turbines, while becoming more efficient, do not have an exponential capacity to become more productive (unlike, say, semiconductors or possibly solar panels using semiconductor materials). Wind turbines are mostly metal structures that require large-scale manufacturing that is in itself potentially polluting.

And because this wind business is, in our view, the most advanced of the renewable sectors, there is already fierce competition for locations, planning permission and for wind turbines themselves, leading to a steady diminution of returns for wind farm operators.

There are some interesting opportunities in development-stage wind farms, particularly in developing economies, but in all fairness we do not regard this as being an area for our *BigIdea* investors to be looking at – this is a capital-intensive business, subject to a lot of government interference and scrutiny, and one where sophisticated investors have already creamed off a lot of the good potential returns.

Far less advanced, and therefore more eligible to constitute one of our ten *BigIdeas*, is **solar power**.

Solar power is with us all the time; there is no place on the planet that is not warmed, to varying degrees, by the power of the sun. The sun is, in effect, a giant nuclear reactor, converting hydrogen into helium, leading to an extremely high surface temperature estimated at 6000° C.

It is that very high temperature which provides us with our solar heat.

Solar radiation on our planet, as one might imagine, is highest near the equator, and receives about 2000 kilowatt-hours per square metre per year at equatorial latitudes. In Northern Europe, this solar radiation falls to about 1000 kw-hours per square metre over a year.

For illustrative effect, it is estimated that it requires about 5 kw-hrs to heat a large bath of water – so when it is sunny in Northern Europe, and for most of the time in the southern states of the US, or in Southern Europe for example, there is plenty of solar radiation available over a relatively small area to satisfy all household demands for electrical and other power. The problem lies in the uneven distribution of the sun's power and in harnessing it.

There are many ways in which the sun's rays – both in the form of direct sunlight and in the form of diffused energy – can be used to generate power, but the extent to which these are successful depends in a large part on the location in which the harnessing takes place, as well as the particular season.

The reason why there is more solar energy at the equator and less at Northern and Southern latitudes is to do with the curvature of the Earth and the consequent angle at which the sun's power strikes the ground. At the equator the land mass receives a wider, direct 'hit' of the sun's power – nearer the poles, it receives less.

In Northern Europe, while the sun's power is relatively strong in the summer months because of the rotational effect of the seasons, in winter much less energy is available. In the southern hemisphere, the same applies, except that the seasons occur in opposition to those in the north.

There are two types of heat generated by the sun on any horizontal surface on earth; one is direct radiation (the sun we SEE), and the other is diffused radiation, or scattered sunlight. In Northern Europe, much of the sun's power over the year comes in diffused form, depending on cloud cover. In Southern Europe, much more comes in the form of direct radiation.

The differences in 'sun power' in Northern Europe between summer and winter are large; in January, it can be only one-tenth of its July average. In Southern Europe, sun power differences are much less pronounced – making solar power a much more viable prospect the further south in Europe that one goes. The same applies to the southern US as opposed to the northern part, or Canada.

There are multitudes of ways in which solar power can be harnessed. We will briefly describe some of the main ones, before settling on what is one of our *BigIdeas* – which is related to the use of cells to generate electricity from the sun's power.

Glass is one of the most obvious and prevalent inventions through which the power of the sun is collected – and its use dates back to Roman times. Increasingly, double, treble or even quadruple glazing is used to 'trap' sun power in houses and buildings, and experiments are under way to use transparent – or glass-like – insulation to achieve the same effect.

By using windows positioned strategically at various points in buildings, almost no matter where they are located in the world, and by employing the latest types of glass material and window construction, we can enhance the amount of heat and light entering a building and reduce leakage back outside the building.

This and other forms of 'passive' solar heating systems are commonplace. Indeed, until the advent of cheap fossil fuel in the US in the early 1900s, many Floridian houses, for example, used solar collectors – simple thermo-siphon systems – to heat hot water.

These types of systems, which use black absorbing surfaces to take in radiation, are returning to popularity. They are quite often joined by such things as heat pipes, so called Trombe walls (a thin glazed air space with thermal storage immediately behind it), and increased use of 'day lighting' (or access for sunlight) in the design of new buildings.

In addition, solar engines and parabolic trough concentrator systems, which have been around for a long time, continue to be experimented with. Solar engines use the sun's power to heat oils, which generate energy to turn turbines, but in practice have proved cumbersome and less efficient than photovoltaic cells.

Parabolic trough concentrator systems use reflective mirrors to heat water to high-steam temperatures, which in turn power an engine to generate electricity.

In fact, the largest solar installation in the world to date is of this type – in the Mojave Desert in California. The latest installation there produces 80 Megawatts using a 464,000 m² collector area of gigantic mirrors. The collectors heat synthetic oil to 390° C, which then produce steam via a heat exchanger. These plants were designed to fuel peak afternoon air-conditioning demands in California, and to some extent have been successful, although the economic returns of this project are highly sensitive to the prevailing price of fossil fuels. These systems are also expensive in terms of initial capital outlay.

The biggest market for any of the types of fairly simple technologies detailed above, especially so-called vacuum solar collectors (which use differential temperatures in tubes to heat water), is in China. There, an estimated 80 per cent of homes heat water in that way. Following close on the heels of the Chinese are the Germans and the Austrians, where generous subsidies exist for all sorts of solar energy.

But the really BIG opportunity in solar power lies elsewhere. The technologies we have described so far generally rely on solar power to produce high heat to drive engines that produce electricity by mechanical effect.

The really big market opportunity lies in direct energy from solar radiation – otherwise known as photovoltaics. This is, put simply, solar energy converted, by means of a solid-state device, directly into electricity.

Photovoltaics is the developing industry which seeks to harness the world's most abundant source of power: the **SUN**.

Net solar input to the earth is more than ten thousand times greater than the world's total use of nuclear and fossil fuels, so if it can be harnessed more efficiently, we literally could be free of ALL types of polluting or dangerous energy.

That, of course, is the nirvana of the renewables industry and many might consider it to be a pipedream. We don't.

We really believe that solar could emerge as an industry to rival any other on the planet over the next 20 years. There are exciting developments under way which make that a possibility.

First, let's briefly describe what the technical basis of this industry is. In principle it's relatively simple.

The word 'photovoltaic' is a combination of the Greek 'photos' (light) with 'volt', the designation for a unit of electromotive force named after the Italian inventor of the battery, Allessandro Volta.

Photovoltaic cells (from now on we will call them PV cells) date back to as far as the 1880s. They employed selenium and were very inefficient compared to today's cells, which typically employ silicon. Less than 1 per cent of the sun's energy hitting those early cells was converted to electricity.

As a result of research carried out in the 1950s at the famous Bell Labs in the US, 'semiconductors' became the basis of solar-related research. Of course, the main use of semiconductors at that stage was in the electronics industry, and particularly in computer technology. But semiconductors have another use, which is now really coming into its own.

Simply put, semiconductors are non-metal materials such as silicon or germanium, whose electrical characteristics lie somewhere between those of a conductive material and an insulating material (which blocks electric flow); hence the 'semi' in semiconductors.

A new method of producing 'doped' material (that is, material with deliberately introduced impurities) was developed at the Bell Labs at that time. This represented the big technological leap forward that has made semiconductor material so useful to us today in the development of a solar industry. This 'doping' altered the electrical behaviour of a semiconductor, making it much more efficient at producing electricity from light.

Over the past 50 years or so, these PV cells – 'doped' semiconductors – have become more efficient and are now typically linked together in modules and then connected to form arrays, which greatly expand their efficiency. These 'evolved' PV cells have now become commonplace.

The use of these PV cells is particularly valuable in powering devices which are in remote locations, where there is no regular supply of electricity. Today, the best silicon solar cells have efficiencies (light to electrical generation) approaching 25 per cent when measured in laboratory conditions, and about 17 per cent in the field. That figure is continuously improving.

As a result, the cost of generating electrical power employing silicon-based PV cells has been significantly reduced.

These types of PV cells work by creating a deficit or a surplus (depending on the doping material) of free electrons – all a bit complex, especially for non-scientists such as ourselves.

By joining materials – some of them containing a surplus and some of them a deficit of free electrons – into what is known as a 'positive-negative junction', an **electrical** field is set up in the region of the junction.

When light falls onto this junction – and light consists of tiny streams of energy called 'photons' – some of that energy is transferred to the junction's material, causing it to move to a higher energy level.

The electrons in the junction then enter an *excited* state where they become freer to move around. Electrons then flow from the 'p' (positive) region to the 'n' (negative) region, thereby creating an electrical current.

In this way electricity is DIRECTLY produced by **the sun's rays shining on the PV cells**.

Until fairly recently, by far the bulk of PV cells were manufactured from **monocrystalline silicon** – a single-strand silicon crystal lattice structure involving an expensive and complex manufacturing process. Recently, new technologies have allowed considerable actual and potential cost reductions in the production of PV cells.

One such advance has been the production of **polycrystalline** PV cells, which are produced by casting ingots of molten silicon. These are less efficient as cells but much cheaper to produce than those made from monocrystalline silicon.

In addition, rather than using solid-state silicon to create PV cells, several companies are now engaged in developing both **thick film** and **thin film** PV 'sheets'.

In **thick film sheets**, polycrystalline films are layered onto ceramic or glass substrates, forming PV modules with an acceptable level of efficiency. Manufacturing costs are still relatively high, however.

But the really exciting developments, in our opinion, are in the **thin film PV** technologies. **Solar cells** can now be made from very thin slices of material, including silicon and compounds of semi-conductors. In the case of silicon, the resulting thin-film is known as **amorphous silicon** (a-Si) in which a much less ordered atomic structure exists than in crystalline silicon. This creates a more complex 'junction' than the 'p' and 'n' junctions of 'conventional' silicon PVs.

Amorphous silicon cells are considerably cheaper to produce than conventional ones, but the resulting efficiency is only about 4–8 per cent in stable field conditions, so the lower cost is generally outweighed by the lesser efficiencies.

However, the production methods by which thin film PVs are made are now being applied in the area that excites us most: compound semiconductors. These manufacturing methods include continuous production at lower temperatures, which requires less energy and less purity, as well as the ability of thin film to be 'laid' cheaply over a wide area.

This is the field of **thin film PV cells produced using compound semiconductors**.

Sounds a bit technical – bear with us, and we will explain. There's money – lots of it – to be made in those PV cells.

Anyway, these 'compound' semiconductors include **cadmium telluride** (CdTe), **copper indium diselenide** (CuINSe$_2$) and most interesting of all **copper indium gallium diselenide** (CIGS). In addition, in some of the newer types of solar panel, silver is sprinkled in small quantities which has a potent effect on improving efficiencies.

CIGS are the most efficient of all of the above with lab efficiency of 17 per cent and in-the-field stable efficiencies achieved of 10 per cent.

CIGS is the most exciting PV technology we can find that is close to full commercialization and it is a technology which brings immediate and tangible cost benefits to the whole solar industry.

It is much closer to commercialization than so-called nanostructure or dye-sensitized PV cells (which are in the future wave of PV technology). By using thin-film manufacturing technology, CIGS production gets away with using only very small amounts of semiconductor material compared with conventional silicon-based wafer PV cell manufacture.

This is because thin-film technology uses **'spattering'** to minimize (expensive) semiconductor use. By using this spattering, the outlay of semiconductor material is reduced from 200 microns to less than 10 as a layer on the 'film'. The cost savings are immense, and the efficiencies are rising, more or less according to the famous Moore's law (doubling every 18 months, a law invented by Gordon Moore, the founder of Intel).

In our opinion, it isn't fanciful to believe that CIGS technology could, in seven or eight years, match almost any form of energy, without subsidy, in terms of cost using a reasonable 'payback' period. Once the systems are installed, then the running and maintenance costs are low.

Companies involved in **CIGS** include Johanna Solar Technology, Odersun and Ascent Solar.

In addition, in high-efficiency PV cells used in such things as spacecraft, where cost is not an issue but reliability is, gallium arsenide as the semiconductor material has been used for some time, and Spectrolab, a division of Boeing, is the leading manufacturer of those types of cells.

These gallium arsenide (GaAs) cells are also being used increasingly in concentrator PV cells, which use mirrors or lenses to concentrate light onto a small area of semiconductor, thereby getting efficiencies of nearly 50 per cent. Gallium arsenide is fairly immune to heat so it is a perfect medium for this, and it is very efficient.

So as we go through this somewhat technical exposition of PVs and their development, readers may see the beginnings of a *BigIdea*.

Solar cells on their own can't be the *BigIdea* – there will be too many players, it is hard to judge which are the better of them, and technological change will obsolete capacity almost as fast as it comes on.

Already, huge amounts of PVs are being produced in China, with a large amount of that destined for Germany. Germany is the world's biggest consumer of PV cells because of the favourable fiscal and monetary regime for solar power in that country.

As an example of the much advanced state of Germany relative to other countries in the use of solar power, Freiburg, a town of just 200,000 people in the Black Forest, has almost as much PV power as the whole of the United Kingdom. Germany has, in total, 200 times as much solar energy output as Britain.

Domestic PV systems in Germany are highly prevalent due to the generous government subsidies available. Without subsidy, a system providing 3 kW of power to a house in Germany currently costs about US$20,000 to install. Prices halved in the seven years from 2000 to 2007 and are expected to halve again in the next seven years.

Today, Germany accounts for half of all the solar PVs installed in the world – representing 2.5 gigawatts of installed capacity. Commentators expect that this figure will rise to 100–150 gigawatts over the next ten years – representing annual growth of over 40 per cent. At that stage, solar power would represent about a fifth of all electricity generation in Germany.

The reason that the German market is growing so fast is because of the so-called feed-in tariff. This means that ANYONE connected to the grid (and that includes private homes) gets a guaranteed payment for putting green electricity into the grid of about four times the market rate – and that goes for solar PV, wind and hydroelectricity.

This feed-in tariff means that anyone installing PV or any other green electricity on their building gets their 'money back' on the systems that they install in about nine years at the current rate – with that payback period falling continuously.

This also means that the Germans have developed a robust renewables industry – with about 250,000 people working in it – and are at the forefront of technological change when it comes to renewable energy.

These feed-in tariffs have the effect of basically putting electricity meters into reverse for the households and industries that have installed the green technologies. In fact, the biggest consumers of PV cells in the world are Bavarian farmers who put solar cells on the roofs of their barns and even in their fields.

Germany has been so aggressive in promoting solar that several world-beating companies have grown up to satisfy the local – and subsidized – domestic demand.

Q-Cells is one example – the company started making PV cells in Germany in 2000 with 19 staff. Today, it has over 1500. It exports half of its product and is the world's second largest maker of PV cells, after Sharp of Japan.

Germany's example is now being copied all around the world, and the effects on the global solar industry will be enormous. Feed-in tariffs have now been adopted by 19 European Union countries and 47 worldwide.

This has all happened since 2004. We find ourselves at the early stages of literally an explosive growth phase in the solar PV industry.

Now, it is certainly true that, without subsidy, solar power is currently less attractive than wind power or certain other forms of renewable energy. For solar to stand on its feet without fiscal or tariff props, using reasonable payback assumptions, oil prices would have to be at about US$140 a barrel. And although we got to that price for oil in mid-2008, it has subsequently slumped back down to US$35 a barrel in line with most other commodities. But that isn't the point. Solar is the most exciting renewable because it is subject to constantly changing technology and to falling prices.

Think of the business as a bit like that of the early personal computer – the early machines were clunky. They didn't do much and really only appealed to geeky early adopters.

Today, this book is written on a computer, as an example; and all of us use the machines for such a wide variety of functions that it would be hard to imagine living without them.

It will be the same with PVs, except that this particular industry has two other compelling features – planetary necessity (solar is about the greenest power imaginable), and government subsidy – which together are kick starting an industry which will be so big as to be almost unimaginable to those of us looking at it today.

OK – so solar will be BIG – but how do we make money from this *BigIdea*?

Well, there are plenty of publicly-quoted solar companies to invest in out there – two good examples are the German companies Q-Cells and Solar World. They aren't particularly undiscovered and have come down sharply in price in the market turmoil of 2008–09. As a result, they now represent much better value for investors.

PV cells are going to be huge – and they all rely on one thing. That one thing is the semiconductor material.

We've written that the 'traditional' PV cells are being supplanted by new thin-film technology which uses compound semiconductor materials.

So one idea is to invest in those materials – but, specifically, in the rare components that are needed to make them.

Eureka!

Let's invest in GALLIUM, INDIUM, GERMANIUM and the other materials which are so vital to this PV story.

There are a number of companies worth looking at in the 'rare semiconductor' material field and we have listed some of them here:

1 **Recyclex** – a French company producing gallium amongst other metals.
2 **New Jersey Mining Company** (symbol: NJMC:US) – produces gallium from mining operations in Idaho, US.
3 **Gold Canyon Resources** (symbol: GCU:CN) – has prospective gallium deposits in Nevada, US. They also have a gold mine.
4 **Bluglass** (symbol: BLG:AU) – Australian producer of gallium nitride.
5 **Dowa Mining** (symbol: 5714:JP) – listed in Japan, it is the world's largest producer of gallium.
6 **AXT INC** (symbol: AXTI:US) – NASDAQ listed, maker of satellite solar panels, mainly producing semiconductor substrates for electronic and optoelectronic uses.
7. **Emerging Metals Limited** (symbol: EML:LN) – has about US$20 million of cash, controlled by Jim and Steve Dattels and will make investments in the field.

Of course there are many other areas to invest in the 'green sector', but we would have to write a very long book to describe them.

Our favourite by far is solar but investors might also look at companies involved in CONSERVATION, WIND POWER and NUCLEAR.

Examples of companies worth looking at in those areas include Fuel Tech, a US company which is working to cut a substantial percentage of carbon emissions from fuel combustion units; Clean Air Power, a London-listed company which is working to get trucks to use natural gas; and Vestas, a Danish company which is one of the world leaders in the production of wind turbines for wind farms – as mentioned above, over 20 per cent of Denmark's electricity comes from wind.

And, of course, there is nuclear. In this area investors might want to look at Niger Uranium, a London-listed company exploring for uranium in Africa, and a spin-off from the now sold Uramin. This company owns a substantial stake in Kalahari Minerals, which holds valuable uranium deposits in Namibia.

There is also the burgeoning market in 'carbon' trading to consider. Increasingly, almost everybody accepts that financial penalties for producing carbon emissions have to be levied if we are to dent their growth.

In Europe, an Emissions Trading Scheme (ETS) has been in operation for a number of years. In this case, the European Union sets a cap on the total amount of tonnage of carbon dioxide that can be emitted EU-wide in any specific period.

The cap is then divided into permits, each allowing the holder to emit one tonne of carbon dioxide. Each country in the EU gets an allocation of permits and then the individual countries allocate them to their main emitting companies, e.g. electricity generating, chemical or manufacturing businesses. Any company not needing its whole allocation is free to sell the surplus in the ETS market and the buyers are typically companies that need more than their allocations.

The idea is that, because there is a value to these permits, companies will be encouraged to invest in 'green' technologies, especially as the 'cap' on total allowable emissions gets progressively lower, making fewer permits available in future years.

This ETS market is supplemented by a variety of other national initiatives in the EU to encourage 'green' behaviour, not all of them successful, but it has to be said that the ETS market is becoming a large and interesting one, however flawed. Investors may wish to consider looking at funds that offer an entry to investing in such permits – one such is Climate Change Capital, listed on the London Stock Exchange.

Although we are not generally great fans of the move to 'biofuels' – crop-based fuels which, in many cases, make very little ecological or financial sense – there is one crop that would be worth investors keeping an eye out for.

This crop is 'Camelina', which is an interesting low-cost feedstock for biodiesel. It has high energy efficiency; is non-food so food production isn't being diverted into energy; uses marginal land which requires no irrigation; is sustainable; and has a very low cost per litre. There are no publicly-available companies in this space as yet but we recommend readers who are interested to keep an eye out for some of them. Please keep a check on www.camelinacompany.com.

Another area of potential interest is waste-to-energy systems. Here, the problems from using landfill sites in many industrialized countries – including the space constraints and the by-production of dangerous methane gas – are leading to an entirely new industry emerging. This is one that seeks to turn waste into energy by burning it, or by using the by-product methane gas (which results from the disposal of any organic waste) to generate heat and electricity.

Around 400 plants in Europe now process 50 million tonnes of municipal solid waste into heat or electricity. This is relatively small in comparison to total waste output, but will grow significantly as a result of governmental and European Union directives which are designed to force change. This growth is being replicated in Japan and in the United States, although as yet to a lesser extent.

Companies involved in the waste industry worldwide which may deserve the closer inspection of our readers include UK companies Shanks and Biffa, both listed on the London Stock Exchange, and involved in landfill site management, waste collection, recycling and disposal. The Japanese company Daiseki, which is that country's only nationwide industrial waste operator, may also be of interest, as are Séché Environnement in France and Lassila Tikanoja of Finland, both involved in new recycling technologies.

Listed companies specializing in converting waste into fuel products include Schmack Biogas from Germany, Plasma Environmental of Canada, and Actelios of Italy.

Yet another area as yet littered with disappointed promise is the fuel cell. This has been in development for some time, with the objective of creating a genuinely electric car with full utility. These fuel cells in development are typically based on hydrogen as a fuel. Hydrogen is attractive because it can be made from all of the sources that electricity can.

At the moment, hydrogen fuel cell powered cars cost about US\$1 million—clearly uneconomical. However, Honda has recently brought out a very promising prototype and it is worth investors taking a preliminary look at Honda shares in Japan or the Honda ADRS in the US.

Perhaps more interestingly, battery technology is beginning to keep pace with the improvements in the rest of the technology industry. Indeed, Elon Musk, a technology entrepreneur, has developed the Tesla, a plug-into-the-wall sports car that uses electricity stored in a lithium-ion battery to create a fast, relatively large-ranged car. But, again, cost is a factor and we believe it will be some time before we see mass commercialization of electric cars, and even then we don't see any great opportunities to make money from them.

Other industries worth keeping an eye on are carbon sequestration and wave/tidal power. The latter is at a relatively early stage but is interesting because in certain parts of the world there is substantial power to be harnessed at river mouth estuaries and around coastal zones. Capital costs are high, but so is predictability of power – wave and tidal patterns are well-established – and it may be that technology developments in this field yield opportunity in the future.

As for the former, carbon sequestration is where carbon dioxide is stored underground, generally in depleted oil and gas fields or in old mines. Statoil, the large Norwegian gas company, has been doing this for many years at its big Sleipner field.

But, as yet, the technology for carbon sequestration is cumbersome and expensive. It has been estimated that if the US sequestered 60 per cent of its carbon emissions, it would take up as much space ANNUALLY as the oil that the US burns to create them takes up in storage.

Not too practical.

But because of subsidy, about 15 power plants are in development in the US which will employ so-called carbon capture (CCS) or carbon sequestration techniques. This is an industry that is capital-intensive, where the economics are dubious, but the end result – the limitation of overall emissions – is positive. It may be one worth keeping a weather eye out for.

But perhaps the one industry – apart from solar – where really exciting things will happen over the next ten years and which may be worth readers' time to research is that of 'energy savings'.

Lighting is one example.

This accounts for about a fifth of all of the world's electricity usage and is largely based on the old-style, inefficient incandescent light bulb. Philips, the big Dutch electricity company, says that a standard bulb costs about US$1 and uses about US$18 dollars of electricity a year. The new low-energy bulbs that are now widely available cost about US$8 but use only US$4 per annum to run – the payback is obvious. And the reduction in carbon emissions if everyone used those bulbs would be huge.

Insulation improvements – space heating takes up more than half of typical power levels used in Northern European, Canadian and US homes – is another area where 'easy' gains can be made in terms of saving electricity.

Energy-saving gadgets could be commonplace within the next few years in all households. Imagine all the computers that are turned on in the world right now. How much energy would be saved globally if each new PC sold came with a fan or cooling device that was just 5 per cent more efficient? The same goes for TVs, fridges, heaters, air-conditioners, etc. With energy savings, it's a numbers game – historically, we haven't really bothered to fine-tune energy consumption of devices because energy supply has not been an issue. But now there are just so many devices in every household that it's really adding to the problem. And of course, every year, more and more households, particularly in the BRIC economies, are becoming 'enfranchised' consumers – i.e. sufficiently affluent and buying devices which further add to pollution.

As a final suggestion for those of you who feel overwhelmed and confused by the sheer volume of opportunities out there and would like to invest in alternative energy in a more general sense, there is an ETF that allows you to do just that. It is called Market Vectors Global Alternative Energy ETF and trades in the US under the symbol GEX. The holdings of the fund range between 1 per cent and 11 per cent per investment. It has certain requirements that a company must meet before the fund invests in it. These are as follows:

- Represent the 30 stocks in the Ardour Global IndexSM (composite) with the highest average trading volume and market capitalization
- Have a market cap exceeding $100 million
- Have a three month trading price greater than $1.00
- Be involved in the business of alternative energy industry (i.e. derive over 50 per cent of total revenues from the industry).

You can read up more about this ETF by visiting www.vaneck.com.

Chapter*Nine*

DiagnosticGrid

Having discussed why securing your financial freedom in later life is essential, and having also explained the types of investments we believe will provide you with a superior rate of return, the next step we will cover is how much you should be investing every month and in which asset classes, given your own unique set of circumstances. Obviously a person who is 50 years old, with no mortgage, children who have already completed their studies and are in the workforce, and a job in senior management will invest very differently from a 30-year-old with a young family and a large mortgage.

Before you can determine (a) how much money you can put away every month, and (b) how much money you are going to need in retirement, we must first take a look at your current financial situation.

Let's start with what, for most people, is the largest monthly outgoing – the mortgage. At the risk of sounding obvious to some of you, your mortgage repayments are typically made up of a repayment of part of the principal (the loan amount) and the interest on the principal. These two amounts are determined by the amount of money you borrowed, the repayment period (such as 25 years) and the cost of borrowing (interest rates).

To help you create your own plan to achieve financial security by the time you wish to stop working, we have developed a *Diagnostic-Grid*, which is a tool designed to extract some key data about your current financial circumstances. From these data, we will be able to recommend an investment plan that is best suited to you.

The type of data that you need to input is:

- Age
- Planned age of retirement (if any)

- Value of existing assets:
  - Cash – all currencies (including cash in money market or time deposit accounts)
  - Equity in the home that you own, if any
  - Stocks
  - Bonds
  - Funds
  - Metals (gold, silver, copper, zinc, etc.)
  - Agricultural and soft commodities (grain, cocoa, sugar, coffee, etc.)
  - Other
- Monthly income (after taxes and other mandatory contributions)
- Monthly payments in rent/mortgage interest
- Average monthly car expenditure (road tax, fuel, insurance, maintenance, loan repayments)
- Balance of outstanding debt plus interest rate charged:
  - Credit cards
  - Mortgages
  - Student loans
  - Personal loans
- Other monthly expenditure, such as:
  - Utilities
  - (Non-car) transportation/travel
  - Telephone/Internet
  - (Non-car) insurance such as medical and life
  - Grocery shopping
  - Entertainment (alcohol, restaurant, cinema, etc.)
  - Education.

Once this type of data is collected, the *DiagnosticGrid* will output the following information:

- Whether you will have sufficient funds to retire.
- The investment monthly mix that we suggest you follow to enable you to reach you retirement financial target. For example, assuming that you have £1000 of cash to invest every month, your allocation may look like this:
  - 17% or £170 into an energy fund
  - 12% or £120 into silver and gold
  - 25% or £250 into a Germany-focused property fund
  - 20% or £200 into a foreign currency basket
  - 14% or £140 into emerging markets/BRIC economies
  - 12% or £120 into a guaranteed equity fund.

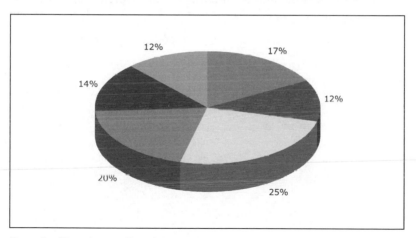

Example of investment allocation

It is worth mentioning that should you end up with less than, say, $100 or £100 for each or some of the *BigIdeas*, it may make more sense to invest quarterly so that the transaction fees associated with making each investment are less than around 4 per cent. For example, it makes no sense to invest $50 into a *BigIdea* each month if the transaction/brokerage fee to make this investment is $20. Investing $500 and paying $20 as a transaction/brokerage fee is more acceptable.

The risk profile of the recommendation will largely be based on the age bracket you fall under. Up to the age of 35, the profile may look like the above example, but there will also be an additional profile provided for 36 to 45, and another one for 46 to 55 and again for 56 to 65. The reason for this is that as one gets closer to retirement age, the appetite for risk should reduce, so the portfolio mix of a 35-year-old will look different to that of a 65-year-old.

Please take a few moments to enter the information in the Microsoft Excel spreadsheet we have created. A copy of this can be found online at www.bigideasbook.com. It is very comprehensive but will only give you accurate information if you feed it with accurate information, so take your time completing it – it's worth it and you will only have to do it once.

Chapter *Ten*

Summary

So there you have it, our message is clear and reiterated many times throughout the chapters – we all need to save a lot more money for retirement than we think for a number of reasons:

- The fact that we're all going to be living longer is an undeniable trend and the massive shortfalls in state pension schemes are clearly reported in many newspapers and books, yet there has been no solution put forward by governments.
- The longer the state pension problem is left unfixed, the more severely it will impact unprepared retirees.
- The prospect of living off our own savings for 20–30 years without a salary or a state pension of any materiality is a rather daunting one and dire consequences await those caught by surprise, so we must be self-reliant in our retirement.

The silver lining in our message is that it's not too late to start taking action, as long as you are at least ten years away from retiring, because time is the key ingredient in compounding returns on our investments – provided we invest in the right things, that is. As the saying goes, time is money, but money can't buy time.

Working your way through the building blocks will not be easy. It will require a great deal of discipline and a change in mindset but it has to be done because it's just not worth investing in *BigIdeas* without making sure that you have a sound investment platform from the outset.

Don't be dismissive about saving and investing, and don't procrastinate about taking steps to building and strengthening your investments. As we mentioned in the introduction, this is just a book; reading it will not automatically add zeros to your bank account balance. Action will.

Patience and perseverance will be rewarded, and once your investment platform is in place, managing your investments will require just one or two hours per month. Investing monthly must become a life practice for the rest of your working life. As we have explained, investing little and often is very effective and doesn't significantly impact your lifestyle. Don't be swayed by general market fluctuations – always take the long-term view, which we believe should be at least ten years. The financial turmoil of 2008 and 2009 has left many stocks and funds trading at multi-year lows. Careful selection of these investments at such depressed prices will mean exceptional returns once the global economy begins to recover by 2010.

To kick things off, you will need to devote at least a weekend to yourself – no phone, no spouse, no kids, and no distractions at all. You need to put together your action plan. Here are some of the things you need to consider in your plan:

- Which building block (page 21) are you starting from? This will determine how ready you are to invest in the *BigIdeas*.
- How long will it take you to work your way through the building blocks? Be realistic but aggressive about your debt repayments.
- When do you plan on retiring?
- Have you prepared your household income statement?
- Have you prepared your household budget?
- Do you have all the information required to complete the *DiagnosticGrid*?
- Are there any unnecessary costs you could reduce from your household budget?
- How much money do you need to get by?
- How much money do you need in retirement? Will you have paid off your mortgage by then?

- What will your life expectancy be when you retire? How many years do you need to fund your life without an income?
- Think about our *BigIdeas* but, more importantly, think of your own *BigIdeas* too. Our book is intended to get you thinking about the world and the way it's changing, and how to profit from that change. There is no doubt that with every revolution of change fortunes are made and lost. Make sure you are on the right side of the next wealth transfer cycle. Remember, even if nine of your *BigIdeas* are mediocre, if the tenth turns into your *MoneyFountain*, your financial freedom is secured for life (provided that you continue to invest and spend wisely, of course).
- Do the research, be structured, take it seriously – you are building the framework for the future of your finances. It's just one weekend in your life and, in the long term, it may very well prove to be the most lucrative two days of your life.
- Find a financial advisor if you don't have one already. Prepare a list of questions to ask. Don't be afraid to ask him/her any questions that may arise from reading this book. Let the financial advisor guide you through the most tax-efficient way to invest in your *BigIdeas*.

It's over to you now: only you can change the state of your financial situation. Best of luck, and remember, be disciplined and think long term.

Glossary

Alpha (α)   A coefficient which measures risk-adjusted performance, factoring in the risk due to the specific stock, mutual fund or portfolio, rather than the overall market.

Baby Boomer   There was a spike in the birth rate immediately after the end of the Second World War up to around 1960. A person born during this period is known as a baby boomer.

Beta (β)   A quantitative measure of the volatility of a given stock, mutual fund, or portfolio, relative to the overall market.

BRIC   Acronym referring to the following countries: Brazil, Russia, India and China.

Dependency Ratio   A ratio calculated by taking the number of retirees and dividing it by the number of workers in a population.

ETF   Electronically Traded Fund. A fund that tracks an index, but can be traded like a stock.

Expense Ratio   Percentage of a fund's assets that the fund manager can withdraw each year to pay for operating expenses.

Float   The number of shares of a company that are actually available for purchase on the stock exchange.

Front Load Usually a percentage, this is the amount charged up front to an investor when buying into a fund. This does not apply to all funds.

GDP Gross Domestic Product. The total value of goods and services produced by a country.

Gross Margin Also known as Gross Profit. It is a company's total sales revenue less the cost of the goods sold.

Inventories The amount of stock that a company has manufactured for resale.

Market Capitalization Sometimes abbreviated to market cap, this is the total value of a company in the relevant currency. It is calculated by multiplying the total number of shares by the price of the share.

NAV Net Asset Value. The total value a fund divided by the number of shares issued.

NYSE New York Stock Exchange

PBV Price to Book Value. Calculated by taking the share price and dividing it by the book value per share.

P/E Ratio or PE Ratio Price to earnings ratio of a company. Calculated by taking the share price of a company and dividing it by the earnings per share.

PEG Ratio Price to earnings to growth ratio. Calculated by taking the PE ratio and dividing it by the company's year-on-year growth rate.

Profit Margin The net income of a company divided by its revenues.

Quick Ratio   A measure of a company's liquidity. It is calculated by taking the company's current assets less inventories and dividing this number by the company's current liabilities.

REIT   Real Estate Investment Trust. This is a company, usually traded publicly, that manages a portfolio of real estate to earn profits for shareholders.

Ticker or Ticker Symbol   Every listed company is assigned an abbreviated form. This can be a letter or letters or even numbers, depending on the exchange.

WTO   World Trade Organization. A global organization that works towards encouraging free trade amongst member states.

Appendix*A*

How to Prepare Your Household Budget

Think of your household as a for-profit corporation. You are its Chief Executive Officer (CEO) as well as being its principal shareholder with your family members. Just like a corporation, you need to understand the financial health of your company (household). In order to do this, you need to complete an income statement and a balance sheet. We have prepared the templates for you. All you need to do is take the time to dig up the paperwork necessary to complete the templates overleaf. For an electronic version of these templates, you can use our *DiagnosticGrid*, which is available for download from www.bigideasbook.com.

If you're not sure how much you spend each month, the best way is to review your bank statements from the past three months and take a monthly average. You can always make adjustments later but this will give you a good starting point and allow you to get a relevant monthly expenditure.

Household Budget Sheet (or Household Income Statement)

Monthly Income (Revenue for your household)	Amount
Salary/salaries (net after deductions)	
Alimony	
Child support	
Other	
TOTAL HOUSEHOLD INCOME	

Monthly Expenses (Household outgoings)	Amount
HOME	
Principal mortgage repayment	
Interest payment on mortgage	
Rent	
Insurance	
Upkeep	
Local taxes/rates/body corporate fees	
Management fees	
UTILITIES	
Telephone (land line and mobile/cell)	
Internet access	
Cable TV	
Electricity	
Gas	
Water charges	

TRANSPORTATION	
Car insurance	
Car fuel (LPG, gasoline, diesel)	
Cark parking/toll charges	
Car maintenance	
Train/bus tickets	
OTHER	
Medical/life insurance	
Other insurance	
Laundry/dry cleaning	
Subscriptions	
Clubs memberships	
Pension scheme	
Groceries	
Eye care/dental care	
DISCRETIONARY SPENDING	
Dining out	
Entertainment (clubs, cinemas, etc.)	
Alcohol and tobacco	
Vacation	
Shopping for clothes/shoes	
Purchases for the home	
Other	
TOTAL HOUSEHOLD OUTGOINGS	
TOTAL AMOUNT AVAILABLE FOR INVESTING (Equals total household income minus total household outgoings)	

Household Balance Sheet

ASSETS		Amount
Cash (savings)		
Investments		
Value of home equity (the part of your home that doesn't belong to the bank)		
Other assets		
TOTAL HOUSEHOLD SAVINGS		
OUTSTANDING DEBT	**Interest rate charged (%)**	**Amount**
Mortgage amount		
Credit cards, store cards, charge cards, etc.		
Car loan		
Personal loan		
Hire-purchase items (instalment plan purchases)		
Student loan		
Other loans		
Other debt		
TOTAL HOUSEHOLD DEBT		

Rearrange this list based on the interest rate charged, the highest rate going to the top of the list. This is the order you should be repaying your debts.

How to Open a Brokerage Account

Before you can invest in any stocks or funds, you need to open an account with a brokerage company. In this day and age, by far the most convenient and cost effective way to do this is to open an account with an online discount broker. This is a very straightforward process. Once you have selected which broker you wish to open an account with, simply click on the 'open account' button and follow the step-by-step instructions.

Here is a list of online brokers that you can open an account with by country. They are in no particular order:

United States

Scottrade	www.scottrade.com
TD Ameritrade	www.tdameritrade.com
Schwab	www.schwab.com
E*Trade	www.etrade.com
Fidelity	www.fidelity.com

United Kingdom

The Motley Fool Share Dealing Service	www.fool.co.uk (select 'Share Dealing' link towards the bottom of the page)
Halifax	www.halifax.co.uk (select the 'Share Dealing' tab from the menu bar)
Selftrade	www.selftrade.co.uk (select 'Open an Account' from the top menu bar)
Interactive Investor	www.iii.co.uk (select 'Register' from the top menu bar)
TD Waterhouse	www.tdwaterhouse.co.uk (select 'Get Started' from the top menu bar)

Worldwide

For the more sophisticated investors who would like to have one account to trade financial markets across the world, we would recommend using Interactive Brokers. The website URL is www.interactivebrokers.com. The account can also be set up to trade in options, futures, bonds and currencies. But be prepared: to open an account you need to complete a rather long and tedious application form.

Appendix *C*

The Top Ten ETF Providers

(As of end December 2008)

	Provider	Assets Under Management ($billion)	% Market Share	Number of ETFs
1	iShares	324.84	45.7	361
2	State Street Global Advisors	146.00	20.5	98
3	Vanguard	45.15	6.4	38
4	Lyxor Asset Management	33.23	4.7	113
5	db x-trackers	24.06	3.4	99
6	PowerShares	22.28	3.1	142
7	ProShares	20.32	2.9	64
8	Nomura Asset Management	14.94	2.1	29
9	Bank of New York	6.69	0.9	1
10	Nikko Asset Management	6.19	0.9	8
	Total	711.0		1,590

Source: Barclays Global Investors, Bloomberg

Index